THIRD EDITION
• • • • • • • •

Racquetball

BASIC SKILLS AND DRILLS

Bill Verner

Mayfield Publishing Company

Mountain View, California
London • Toronto

Library of Congress Cataloging-in-Publication Data

Verner, Bill.
  Racquetball: basic skills and drills/Bill Verner. — 3rd ed.
    p. cm.
  ISBN 1–55934–073–8
  1. Racquetball.   I. Title.
  GV1003.34.V47   1991
  796.34'3 — dc20   91–22393
                             CIP

Manufactured in the United States of America

10 9 8 7 6 5 4 3 2 1

Mayfield Publishing Company
1240 Villa Street
Mountain View, California 94041

Sponsoring editor, James Bull; production editor, Sondra Glider;
manuscript editor, Ellen Kurek; text and cover designer, Richard
Kharibian; photographer, Sena Zimmer; illustrator, Guy Magallanes;
cartoonist, Kevin Opstedal. Cover photo: © David Madison 1991. The
text was set in 10/12 Palatino by TypeLink and printed on 50# Butte
des Morts by Banta Company.

Racquetball rules in the Appendix are reprinted by permission of the
American Amateur Racquetball Association.

CONTENTS

● ● ● ● ● ● ● ●

PREFACE

I have been extremely gratified by the success of the first two editions of *Racquetball: Basic Skills and Drills*. My goals have been the same in each edition: to provide beginners with the basics they need to play and enjoy racquetball, and to include enough information to help more advanced players refine their strokes and improve their playing strategies.

A key factor in racquetball's popularity is its lifetime health and fitness benefit. Racquetball games provide thorough cardiovascular workouts in less than an hour. People who play regularly benefit from lower levels of body fat, increased stamina, and improved muscle tone. Because the beginning skills are easily learned, everyone can enjoy playing racquetball after just a few basic lessons.

This new edition includes the following features:

- A three-part organization, allowing students to focus on shots and strategies appropriate for their level of expertise.

- A wide variety of drills, which are provided immediately after each stroke or strategy is described.

- Two kinds of boxes: "Hints for Improvement," offering practical tips for better play, and "Common Faults," to help students avoid errors.

- More than 130 photographs and line drawings that clearly illustrate important concepts, equipment, and strategies.

- A new chapter (10) on racquetball as part of an overall fitness program.
- The latest rules and safety information.

I would like to thank the following reviewers for their valuable suggestions: Gerald Carlson, University of Southwestern Louisiana; Patrick R. Cobb, Georgia Southern University; Patricia Hughes, University of Texas, Arlington; and D. Michael Morris, Tarrant County Junior College.

Introducing Racquetball

1

⋯⋯⋯

HISTORY

Racquetball is a relatively recent sports phenomenon. Although it evolved from a number of racquet sports, it is most directly related to paddleball.

Today's version of racquetball began in the early 1950s and is generally credited to Joe Sobeck, who designed a short tennis racquet, or paddle racquet with strings. He called his new sport "paddle rackets." As the equipment improved, racquetball as we know it today emerged.

Racquetball's first premier players included Bud Meuhleisen and Charles Brumfield, who used control, strategy, and finesse to become national champions. Racquetball's modern era began with Marty Hogan, who introduced a totally new concept in racquetball strategy — power racquetball. In his time he was the hardest hitting player alive and won many national championships with sheer power.

Over the past few decades, the greatest advances in racquetball have resulted from the tremendous technological improvements in racquets. Racquets have evolved from the basic wood model to today's complex models made of space-age materials and featuring oversized heads.

Numerous organizations have also influenced the development of racquetball. Currently the sport's governing body is the American Amateur Racquetball Association (AARA), which has been promoting the sport since 1968 and is officially recognized by the U.S. Olympic Committee.

1

PREGAME BASICS

Types of Courts

Racquetball can be played on one-, three-, or four-wall courts. The most popular of these is the enclosed, four-wall court with a ceiling. However, at the middle and senior high school levels, one- and three-wall courts are more common than the more expensive four-wall style court.

This book deals mainly with four-wall play, but most of the principles you will learn here can also be used in one- and three-wall courts.

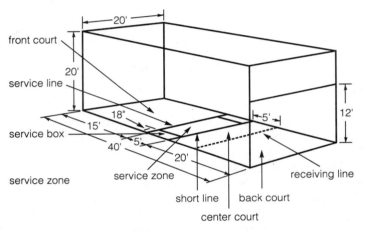

Regulation four-wall court.

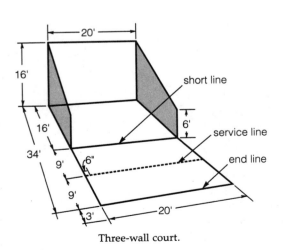

Three-wall court.

One-wall court.

The walls of racquetball courts may be made from various materials, including cement and prefabricated fiber-resin panels. Four-wall courts may be constructed of glass for better viewing by spectators. Official indoor courts have wooden floors, although schools often select cement as a less expensive alternative.

A Few Rules

The object of the game is simple—get to the ball before it bounces on the floor twice, and then hit it to the front wall on the fly.

Racquetball can be played by two, three, or four players. **Singles** and **doubles** are played in club and **tournament** competition. **Cutthroat** is played with three players—a server who plays against two receivers. When the server loses the rally, another player earns the **serve**. **Cutthroat** is often played in racquetball clubs and on school courts.

To start the game, the server stands in the service zone, bounces the ball, and strikes it so it hits the front wall and rebounds into the court anywhere beyond the **short line**.

On the serve, the ball may hit only one side wall and must strike the front wall first. A serve that first hits the front wall and then either the back wall or ceiling is a **fault** and is replayed. Serves that hit two side walls or do not travel beyond the short line are also faults and are replayed. If a served ball hits any other surface before it strikes the front wall, the server loses his serve.

Most courts have a **receiving line** marked on the court. The receiving line is a line parallel to the short line and five feet behind it. The area between the short line and the receiving line is called the **safety zone**. The receiver may not enter the safety zone to return the serve until the ball bounces.

After the ball passes the short line and bounces, the receiver must return the ball to the front wall before it bounces on the floor twice. Unlike the serve, the return may hit any number of walls first, as long as it eventually hits the front wall before hitting the floor. The players then hit the ball alternately. The ball may be hit in the air before it bounces; however, it must be hit and returned to the front wall before it bounces twice. Additionally, the ball can take any route to the front wall, hitting the ceiling, front, and side walls in any combination.

Scoring Only the server or the serving team can score **points**. If the receiver wins the **rally**, the receiver gains the serve and the opportunity to score.

At present, several different scoring systems are used. However, the official AARA rules state that a **game** is won by the first side to accumulate 15 points. A **match** is won by the first side to win two games. When each side wins one game, the third game is played until one side first accumulates 11 points. There is no deuce game, overtime, or win-by-two-points rule as in Ping-Pong or tennis.

The AARA encourages players to try different scoring systems to adapt to quicker play, as in college and recreational class matches. Additionally, the AARA has adopted the modified "no bounce" rule for juniors under eight years of age. Playing by this rule is an excellent way for beginners to learn the sport without the frustration of trying to hit the ball after only one bounce. Try playing this way until you have acquired the skill and quickness to play the game the hard way.

Safety Hinders Since racquetball is played in a confined area, certain precautions should be taken. You should *always stop your swing if there is any possibility of hitting your opponent* with either the racquet or the ball! In all cases that might result in injury, the word **hinder** should be called out and the rally replayed. The additional hinder rules written into the regulations should also be understood before beginning play.

Etiquette

Racquetball is meant to be enjoyed. Observing court etiquette not only makes the game more enjoyable, it also makes it safer. Remember the following pointers while playing racquetball:

1. Good sportsmanship is the foundation of racquetball etiquette. Treat others as you would like to be treated.
2. Your practice period should not exceed five minutes. On the other hand, don't rush your opponent into starting the game.
3. Wait until your opponent is ready before serving.

4. Call out the score (server's score first) before each first serve. This will help avoid confusion and argument and help the game continue smoothly.

5. Be careful not to overswing on the court. It can cause injuries.

6. Talk only when necessary during the match and never while your opponent is making a shot. However, acknowledge a good shot by your opponent. In doubles, it is permissible to help your partner by calling for certain shots.

7. Work at controlling your temper. Banging your racquet against the walls and the floor is dangerous and can be expensive.

8. Be fair on your calls and shots. If your shot "skips in" and your opponent does not see it, call it against yourself. Fair play leads to friendship on and off the court.

9. Give your opponent a fair chance to return the ball. Don't intentionally block his view.

10. Don't crowd or push your opponent. The closer you get to your opponent, the greater the chances of getting hit, either with the ball or the racquet.

11. Call all hinders! If you feel there is any possibility of hitting your opponent, don't swing. Play the point over.

12. After the match, thank your opponent. Congratulate him if he won.

WARMING UP

Racquetball is a very demanding, physical sport. It is important to spend at least ten minutes warming up before you begin playing. There are many exercises that can be done to loosen your muscles. Pick those that you feel are good for you and do them before playing. Sample exercises include arm-circles, wrist curls, push-ups, elbow contractions, trunk twists, toe-touches, knee and back bends, hamstring and groin stretches, skipping rope, and light jogging. This is only a partial list and there are many more, but the idea is to warm up properly to speed up your metabolism, increase your heart and lung action, and limber up your joints for movement to prevent injuries.

Racquets are made with many designs and materials. Try several before making a final choice.

EQUIPMENT

The Racquet

Today racquets are made primarily of aluminum, injection-molded composite, or hand-laid composite. There are many shapes and designs. The most popular, however, are the teardrop (closed-mouth or round) and rectangular shapes.

Size Today's racquets come in a wide variety of sizes and shapes. Racquet head sizes can generally be categorized as either standard/midsized or oversized.

The oversized racquet head frames tend to offer a larger "sweet spot," providing a larger hitting area that results in a higher margin for error on off-center hits. They can yield greater power too, but this is usually a function of racquet flex and string tension. Midsized racquet head frames usually offer more control and better maneuverability.

Power and control are greatly affected by string tension and racquet flexibility no matter what size head the racquet has. Greater power is associated with low string tension and high flexibility, whereas greater control is associated with low flexibility and high string tension. Of course, control is of primary importance, and power should only be added after control is mastered. A beginner will not be able to notice much difference between racquets of different sizes, string tensions, and flexibilities; however, as your skills improve, you should experiment with many racquets to select one that fits your goals and abilities.

Weight The racquet must be light enough to allow a fast swing and a fast reaction time. A light racquet also reduces arm fatigue. However, it must not be so light that it doesn't propel the ball with force. Racquets today typically weigh between 225 and 270 grams (8 to 9½ ounces). Racquets fall into the following weight categories:

Light: 225 to 240 grams (8 to 8½ oz.)

Medium: 240 to 255 grams (8½ to 9 oz.)

Heavy: 255 to 270 grams (9 to 9½ oz.)

Handle Grips   The circumference of the racquet handle determines the size of the **grip**. The wrist is used extensively in racquetball. Don't get a racquet with a grip that's too large, because it will greatly reduce your hitting power and wrist snap. If you play tennis, a good way to select the correct handle grip is to choose a grip that feels too small. Grip sizes usually range between 3¼ inches and 4¼ inches.

Composition   There are three main types of racquets: hand-laid composites, injection-molded composites, and aluminum. Composite racquets are made of fibers such as fiberglass, graphite, boron, and Kevlar and are combined with special plastics that give stiffness and flexibility without adding extra weight.

Hand-laid composites offer the highest level of racquet performance. Long, continuous fibers are laid in a racquet frame in various combinations, amounts, locations, and angles. Features such as stiffness, flexibility, weight, and balance can be controlled through this process.

Injection-molded composite frames offer more flexibility than hand-laid composites. This is because they are made by injecting composite fibers into specially designed racquet molds.

Aluminum racquets have the most durable frames and maintain consistent playability and feel throughout the frame.

All these types of racquets perform differently. Before you purchase a racquet, try several brands. Pick them up and swing them a few times, testing their grip, weight, and balance. *Racquet choice is mostly a matter of personal preference.* Make sure it feels good before you buy it.

Hints for Improvement

Beware of injection-molded racquets that claim to contain "graphite." Graphite by itself does not automatically make a racquet good. It's the process by which it is introduced into the racquet that counts.

Strings   Nearly all racquets are strung with nylon. Nylon is relatively cheap, lasts a long time, and is resilient.

The tension of the strings determines the "bounce" of the ball off the racquet. Players' preferences vary, but racquets are generally strung with between 25 and 50 pounds of tension.

Eye Guards

Eye guards or prescription athletic glasses are highly recommended for racquetball play. Serious eye damage, even loss of sight, can be caused by balls traveling at speeds up to 120 mph, or by the edge of a racquet. Professionals wear eye guards during practice as well as competition and advocate their use. Eye guards are also mandatory in all tournament competition. *You should wear eye protection at all times.*

Balls and racquets can cause serious eye damage. Use eye protection at all times.

The Ball

There are a number of good brands of balls manufactured today. Stick to a name brand that has been approved by the AARA.

Gloves

Many players wear gloves to help prevent the racquet from slipping. A wide variety are available. Choose the one you find most comfortable.

Dress

The only dress requirement for racquetball is comfortable, well-fitting clothes. Shorts and a light shirt or tee shirt are recommended. Women usually wear shorts. You should wear shoes that do not mark the floors, preferably white-soled shoes.

For tournaments, your clothing must be light in color, because dark clothes can camouflage the ball. Head- and wristbands help keep perspiration out of your eyes and off your hands.

Forehand and Backhand Grip

2

GRIPPING THE RACQUET

Of all racquetball fundamentals, nothing is more basic than the way you grip the racquet. Your grip determines how and where you hit the ball as it makes contact with the strings.

The racquet handle can be divided into eight edges or "bevels." If your racquet handle is round and does not have these edges, imagine that the handle is divided into these eight areas.

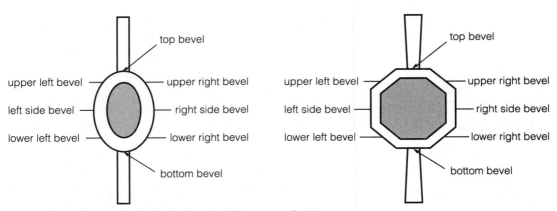

Bevels. View is from end of butt, looking straight up toward strings.

All grip and stroke instructions are written for right-handed players, so if you're left-handed you'll have to reverse the instructions.

BASIC FOREHAND GRIP

When gripping the racquet, it is most important that it *feel* comfortable in your hand. You can form the basic grip used for hitting forehand shots by "shaking hands" with your racquet. The "V" formed by your thumb and index finger should run down the middle or slightly to the left of the middle of the racquet.

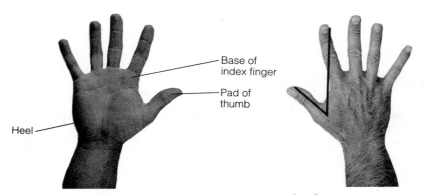

Check the position of these key points on your hand as you experiment with basic racquet grips. Left: key palmar points. Right: "V" crease between thumb and forefinger.

Heel of hand on the upper right bevel.
Pad of thumb on the left side bevel.
Base knuckle on the right side bevel.
The "V" of your hand should be in the middle or slightly to the left of the middle top bevel when forming the basic forehand grip.

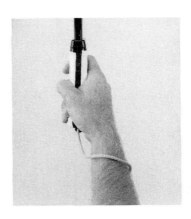

Shake hands with your racquet to obtain the proper forehand grip.

BASIC BACKHAND GRIP

To obtain the basic **backhand** grip, turn your hand counter-clockwise from the forehand grip until the knuckle of your index finger is on top of the handle.

Heel of hand on top bevel.
Pad of thumb diagonally across the lower left and left side bevels.
Base knuckle on the top or slightly to the right of the top bevel.
The "V" of your hand should be in the middle of the left side bevel when forming the basic backhand grip.

When the ball hits the racquet, the racquet face should be perpendicular to the floor and parallel to the front wall. If you use the basic forehand grip, you must switch your grip to a backhand grip to hit a backhand shot. Otherwise, unless you tilt your wrist forward, the racquet face will be tilted backward when you contact the ball. The result will be a weak shot hit too high onto the front wall.

During a rally, you must change to the appropriate grip. Like most racquetball fundamentals, grip adjustment becomes a habit with practice.

Most Common Faults
1. The fingers are too close together in a "fist" grip.
2. The hand is too high or low on the racquet grip.
3. The thumb should be wrapped around the racquet so that it almost touches your fingers. Don't put your thumb on the top of the racquet.

3......

Fundamentals and Drills

STROKE TECHNIQUE

Racquetball is a combination of stroke technique and wrist action. In addition to the wrist action involved, you'll find that you can master the stroke technique with just a little practice.

Focus on the following five maneuvers when learning any stroke. Several maneuvers have been broken down into parts for easier explanation. Even though we speak of the swing as if it consists of separate parts, *the stroke must be one smooth, continuous motion.*

1. Ready position
     Stance
     Grip

2. Backswing
     Pivot
     Body angle
     Set position
     Weight distribution
     Moving to the ball

3. Forward swing
     Weight transfer and hip and shoulder rotation
     Point of contact
     Racquet and body position

4. Follow-through

5. Recovery to ready position

Complete forehand stroke.

Complete backhand stroke.

The ready position.

Because the principles for forehand and backhand shots are almost identical, the following discussion applies to both of them (except when specifically noted).

Ready Position

Before each forehand or backhand shot, you must assume the **ready position**. Place your feet about shoulder-width apart (1) with your knees slightly flexed (2) and your weight balanced equally on the balls of each foot (3). Your back should be bent slightly (4) and your head should be up (5). Your racquet is held in front of you (6) with a comfortable bend at your elbows. Hold the racquet with your forehand grip.

From this position, you can move in any direction and hit any stroke. After every shot, attempt to set up your ready position at **midcourt** just behind the short line.

Hints for Improvement

1. Put more weight on your toes than on your heels. Don't stand "flat-footed."
2. Bend your knees, bounce up and down, and relax. Stiff or straight knees usually indicate that you're tense.
3. Hold your racquet at waist level, midway between high and low shots. If you hold it too high or too low, you might not be able to adjust in time.

Forehand pivot.

Backhand pivot.

Backswing

The essence of a good forehand or backhand is early preparation, which begins with the **backswing**. An early backswing allows you to react to unusual bounces, to stroke the ball properly, and to hit a greater number of offensive shots. The backswing should begin as soon as you can tell whether the ball is coming to your forehand or backhand, and preferably before it strikes the floor. As soon as you can determine the ball's direction of approach, you should adjust your grip (if necessary) and pivot your body, which aids your backswing.

Forehand Pivot   The hips (7) and shoulders (8) turn 90 degrees so that they are parallel to the side walls. The feet merely twist in place (9).

Backhand Pivot   The procedure is reversed. Turn your hips and shoulders. The body turn is a little greater on the backhand; you should almost be looking at the front wall over your front shoulder (8).

Set Position   After the hips and shoulders have pivoted, take a step forward with your front foot (10) (left foot for forehand, right for backhand). Your entire body should now be facing the side wall. Whenever you have to run to hit the ball, always try to be in the proper set position before swinging. Make sure your knees are comfortably bent and your feet are not too far apart. In the set position, the racquet should be pointed at the ceiling (11) with the arm bent ap-

Forehand set position.

Backhand set position.

proximately ninety degrees and the upper arm parallel to the floor. The wrist should always be in a cocked position ready to "snap" when you hit the ball.

Weight Distribution   While pivoting during the forehand stroke, your weight initially should be on the right foot (for the backhand it's the opposite). As you step forward, your weight begins to transfer from the rear foot (12) to the foot stepping forward (13).

Moving to the Ball   Once you have pivoted, you must move to the exact location on the court where you can meet the ball squarely. The success of this action depends upon quick and accurate judgment, which can only be gained through experience.

Weight transfer: All weight should be on your front foot at contact.

Hints for Improvement

1. Try to start your backswing before the ball reaches the service box. Advanced players begin their backswing early; beginners often wait until the ball is too close to them.

2. Maximum power and best form result from turning your hips and shoulders sideways (facing the sidewall) during stroke preparation. Don't face the front wall while preparing your stroke: Pivot!

3. Make sure the top of your racquet points toward the ceiling in the preparation phase. This results in greater power. Don't point it toward the back wall.

4. The power of the stroke comes from snapping your wrist. When bringing your racquet back, flex your wrist and prepare to "snap" it when you hit the ball.

5. During your stroke, transfer your weight from the back foot to the front foot. Don't keep all the weight on the back foot. Get the momentum going forward!

6. When hitting the ball, place your feet about shoulder-width apart. Don't overstride or you'll fall off balance.

7. Take a big swing! Don't keep your arm close to your body. Let it flow.

Backhand position.

Forward Swing

Rotate hips and shoulders upon contact.

Weight Transfer and Hip and Shoulder Rotation The forward swing should start with your weight shifting from the back foot to the front foot. As you transfer your weight, your shoulders and hips should begin to rotate toward the front wall. This rotation is easier if you bend your back leg inward (14) and slightly toward the floor.

Point of Contact For the forehand stroke, your elbow should lead as you begin the downward arc of your swing (15). The ball should come in contact with your racquet at a point opposite the instep of your front foot (16). For the backhand stroke, the **point of contact** should be about 6 inches in front of your instep, or just before the ball reaches your front foot (17).

The elbow leads the forehand stroke.

Point of contact: forehand and backhand.

For a powerful shot on both the forehand and backhand, snap the wrist forward (18) as ball contact is made. This snap should be firm, not flimsy, facilitating an accurate shot. The snapping of the wrist during the forehand stroke can be com-

Snap the wrist at the point of contact for a powerful stroke.

pared to the wrist action that characterizes throwing a baseball or skipping rocks, and to that which characterizes throwing a frisbee or snapping a towel for the backhand.

Hints for Improvement

1. A stroke is made with *both* arms and body. Don't use just your arms while hitting the ball. Rotate those hips!

2. Try to keep your eyes on the ball. Most beginners turn their head to see where the ball is going to go before it's hit.

3. Once the ball gets behind your front foot, you'll lose most of your power upon contact. Try to hit every ball when it's in front of your front foot.

4. Advanced players hit the ball close to the floor. Therefore, check to see if your knees are bent when you finish the stroke. If your knees are straight, you're hitting the ball too high.

5. When hitting forehand and backhand **kill shots**, keep the racquet face perpendicular to the floor at its point of contact. If the hitting surface is tilted toward the floor, your shots are likely to go into the floor. If the hitting surface is tilted toward the ceiling, your shots will go too high.

6. Remember, the forehand and backhand shots are hit with different sides of the racquet. Beginners often hit a backhand with the forehand side.

7. The stroke is a whipping motion—snap your wrist and elbow. Don't hit the ball with a firmly locked arm, as in tennis.

Your follow-through will tell you how good your stroke was.

Follow-Through

The **follow-through** should be practiced along with all the other parts of the swing. It will add power to your stroke and put you in a better position to handle the next shot. Let your racquet arm swing naturally across your body after ball contact is made. Try to finish your stroke ''high'' (19).

At the completion of the follow-through, you should be well balanced, not falling over. To do this, you need to check your body for several key things. Your body should be bent low and your eyes still focused on the ball (20). Your front knee should be slightly bent (21), and your back knee should be at an almost ninety-degree angle (22). Your front foot should be flat on the floor (23), and your shoulders and hips should be rotated facing the front wall (24). To help execute this rotation, your back heel should be raised, with the toes scraping the floor (25).

Hints for Improvement

1. Stay loose. Bend the knees when hitting the ball. Don't tighten up or get stiff.
2. Follow through completely. This gives you power and fluid motion. Beginners tend to stop the stroke right after contact. This sudden jerking stop can cause tendinitis and a sore elbow.
3. Always try to be balanced at the end of the stroke. Don't rise up on your toes on contact.

Recovery

Return quickly to the ready position by swinging your right foot around and parallel to your left. You are now prepared to hit a ball coming toward either side of your body.

PRACTICE DRILLS FOR FOREHAND AND BACKHAND

Drills must be practiced and repeated regularly to improve your game. Although there are hundreds of drills to practice, the following can help break the monotony while improving your skills. As you learn different drills, select those you enjoy the most and practice them regularly.

● Beginning Stage Drill

The primary objective at this point is to perfect your technique. Stand in **centercourt**.

With your free hand, drop the ball gently in front of you from waist height.

Wait for the ball to bounce. As it drops down to knee level, execute a low forehand to the front wall. Bend your body into the shot. Step toward the ball and make contact with the ball as low as possible. Snap your wrist for extra power.

Drop the ball and hit ten shots with good form and balance.

Be your own teacher after every shot. Compare your form to that exhibited by the players in the pictures in this chapter. The best way to analyze your form is to *"freeze" at the end of your stroke*. This enables you to check to see how well you executed the swing *during* the stroke. Are you balanced, with good follow-through? Is your position similar to that of the players in the illustrations in this chapter? Once you attain good form, repeat the drill again until you can hit ten consecutive kill shots (shots in which the ball must hit no higher than six inches from the floor) while maintaining good form and balance.

Before moving to the intermediate stage, the ten kill shots should be executed from midcourt, then from **backcourt**.

After mastering the forehand stroke, repeat this drill using the backhand stroke.

• Intermediate Stage Drill

You should have perfected your mechanics and technique in the beginning stage drill. In this stage, concentrate on accuracy as well as form.

The intermediate stage drill is the same as the beginning stage drill, except targets are placed along the front wall. Evenly space five or six plastic tennisball tubes (or use racquetball tubes for a greater challenge) along the front wall. When you can hit three tubes out of ten shots from both the midcourt **and** backcourt with the forehand **and** backhand stroke, you're ready for the advanced stage drill.

Use tubes as targets for both backhand and forehand drills.

• Advanced Stage Drill

1. Start your drill in midcourt. Place one tube against the front wall. Drop and hit ten shots using good technique. When you can hit the tube three times out of ten shots with your forehand and backhand, advance to the next level of this drill.

2. Set up several tubes along the front wall as in the intermediate stage drill. Move to backcourt, and drop and hit ten shots with your forehand and backhand. Advance to the next level of this drill when you can hit three tubes with your forehand and three with your backhand.

3. Stay in backcourt and toss the ball at the *side walls*, repeating the procedure outlined in level 2. Let the ball drop to shin height before making contact. Hitting three out of ten with both strokes moves you to the next level.

As you get better, toss the ball off the side and back walls to practice your shots.

4. Repeat the drill in level 3, but toss the ball off the **backwall**.

5. When you can master all the above levels (dropping and tossing off the side and back walls), set up just one tube as you did in level 1. Remain in backcourt and again toss the ball off each of the walls, hitting forehand and backhand shots. Out of ten shots, use the following scoring system to grade your hits:

Scoring

0–1	You need practice; go back to level 1 and start over.
2–3	You're a good player.
4–7	You're a serious player, rated excellent.
8–10	You're an expert. Think of joining the "pro" circuit. You can make a living at this game.

• Sharp-Shooter Stage Drill

1. Stand in backcourt. Hit the ball to the front wall using good form and return to the ready position. As the ball rebounds off the front wall and comes toward you, hit a kill shot. Practice both forehand and backhand kill shots. Repeat this level to see how many times you can execute a perfect kill shot. Use the advanced stage drill chart to rate yourself.

2. For an additional challenge, add one tube to the front wall, repeat as in level 1, and score yourself again.

• Additional Forehand and Backhand Drills

Hitting off the Front Wall

This drill develops your ability to respond to a ball that is hit off the front wall.

Begin in centercourt and hit or throw the ball so that it hits high up on the front wall. The ball should rebound to the floor and come back toward you quite low. Move forward as needed and execute a **pinch** kill **shot**. Repeat the drill, this time executing a **down-the-line pass shot**.

This drill can be repeated for all front-wall shots, including the **straight kill**, pinch kill, down-the-line pass, and **cross-court pass shots**.

After perfecting this drill, move to various positions on the court and gently hit the ball off the front wall. Move into position and execute good shots. Concentrate on form and accuracy using both forehand and backhand.

• Hitting off the Back Wall

Stand in the backcourt close to the back wall. While standing sideways, toss the ball off the back wall and try to hit it *before it bounces*. When you perfect this, hit the ball hard and high on the front wall so that after bouncing on the floor it hits the back wall. Practice shuffling back and setting up to hit the ball before it hits the floor.

Toss the ball off the back wall and hit it before it bounces.

4

Basic Serves and Service Return

The only time you are not rushed, running, exhausted, or crashing into walls while trying to hit a shot is when you are serving. Therefore, relax, take control, and plan a good serve that will put you on the offensive and your opponent off balance.

The serve is the only time you can be assured of having total command of the ball. It is your best opportunity to execute a strong shot. Your hope is that your serve will be so strong that your opponent will be unable to return it. This is called an **ace**.

In actual play against a competent opponent, however, you must expect that your opponent will be able to return many serves. Consequently, you should try to serve so that if your opponent does manage a return, it is a weak one. You should then be in position to take advantage of the weak shot and score.

PRACTICE

At first, practice alone on a court. Simply stand in the appropriate position and hit serves. *Practice each serve separately until you master it.* Watch to see where the ball makes contact with the front wall and where it rebounds. Always work toward better serves. Practice so that your serves come naturally and instinctively.

After mastering a few serves, practice hitting serves and serve returns with a partner. Set up as though you were in regular play. Hit the serve and observe its course to see how effective you were.

Your partner will try to make the best return on the serve. Instead of rallying, though, your partner should observe the ball to see how effective his return was.

Then set up and try it again. By rotating service and service return, you can practice both quickly.

Fifteen minutes of concentrated, intense practice can accomplish more than hours of relaxed, nonchalant drills and practice.

You should continue your practice in games. Though you certainly want to play to win, you might also want to work on your service. Depending on your opponent, your match can become a strong learning experience for both of you.

SERVICE RULES

The serve is started from anyplace within the service zone. No part of either foot may extend beyond either line of the service zone. Stepping on, but not over, the line is permitted. The server must remain in the service zone from the moment the service motion begins until the served ball passes the short line. Violations are called **foot faults**. Always call the score before you serve, giving the server's score first.

Begin the serve by bouncing the ball to the floor while standing within the confines of the service zone. Hit the ball so it strikes the front wall first and hits the floor on the re-

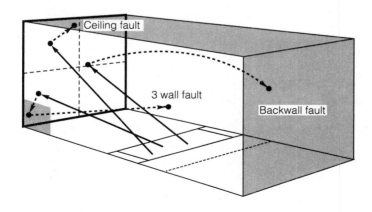

Fault serves. Two faults result in an "out." Any serve that does not hit the front wall first is an "out."

bound behind the back edge of the short line, touching or without touching a side wall. If a service ball hits three walls without touching the floor first, it is a fault. A serve that first hits the front wall and then the ceiling or back wall without touching the floor is also a fault.

All serves must hit the front wall first or else you lose the serve. A balky serve or a fake swing at the ball is counted as an "out." Don't serve until the receiver is ready.

A screen serve is a serve that passes so close to the server or server's partner in doubles that it prevents the receiver from having a clear view of the ball. You must allow the receiver a clear view of the ball when serving. In casual play, a screen serve can be taken over; however, official rules (4.10i) state that a screen serve is a fault.

THE CENTERCOURT POSITION

The player who commands the **centercourt** *position is most often the winner.* However, in advanced racquetball, you learn to position yourself for the best return anywhere on the court. Nevertheless, centercourt is usually the most important position. When you serve, *you* begin in centercourt. You are in a position to force your opponent to make a weak or low-percentage return by driving your opponent out of centercourt.

Don't give your opponent the opportunity to guess what serve you are going to hit. Either hit all your serves from the same position, or else hit serves from many different positions in the service box. The object is to disguise your serves. Don't get into a pattern that allows your opponent to anticipate your serve.

Some serves can either make for a weak return or force your opponent out of centercourt, or do both. A good player aims to master serves that result in weak returns.

THE THREE BASIC SERVES

The three basic serves are the **drive**, the **Z-serve** (see Chapter 6: Advanced Serves and Serving Strategy), and the **lob**. When you perfect all three of these serves, you will probably win most of your games. The most important basic serve in racquetball is the drive serve.

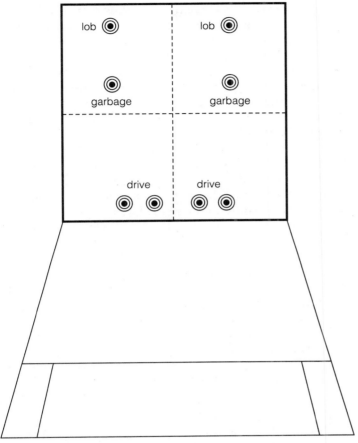

Serve targets.

Many players depend on the drive, but there are two reasons why it is essential for a good player to develop a variety of shots. The first is that if you have several different serves, your opponent can't set up each time by knowing what you're going to serve.

Second, if you keep repeating the same serve over and over, you give your opponent so much practice that he or she becomes adept at returning that serve.

Thus a mixed bag of serves is an essential strategy.

The Drive Serve

You will use the drive serve more than any other. It is a powerful serve. Top players may use it as much as seventy per-

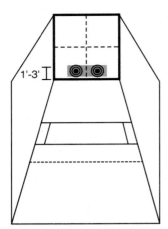

Target area for drive serves: one to three feet high just off center.

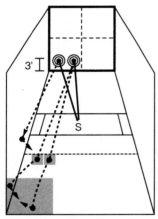

Typical drive serve trajectories (one side shown). Hit to both sides!

cent of the time. Hit the ball hard and low off the front wall, forcing the receiver to react very quickly. This makes it difficult for your opponent to get to the ball for the return.

Although this is the most frequently used serve, it is a hard one to properly execute. The drive serve must hit the front wall low and near the center, which causes the ball to ricochet toward the back corner. If hit accurately, it is highly effective in keeping your opponent off balance, guessing where the ball will rebound.

A strong drive serve is an essential part of every good player's repertoire. You should be able to hit a drive either to the left or right with equal effect. This forces your opponent to wait for the serve in the center of the court. If you hit drive serves predominantly to the right, for example, your opponent will move a bit to the right, giving your opponent an advantage in getting to the shot for a return.

The drive serve lines, which form the drive serve zone, are parallel with the side walls. The lines are located three feet from the side wall. Any drive serve down-the-line must start outside of this line. However, the serve may pass through this zone after rebounding off the front wall.

There are three elements to consider with the drive serve — (1) your body's position when your racquet contacts the ball, (2) the spot you are aiming for on the front wall, and (3) the ball's anticipated return trajectory.

1. *Contacting the ball.* In the drive serve, strive for power, as well as accuracy. You will obtain the greatest power when you hit the ball fairly low (usually at shin height). As indicated earlier, both body rotation and balance are essential. Shift your weight to your front foot just as you make contact. This puts your weight "into the ball."

2. *Target.* You have two goals in targeting the ball. One is to see that it rebounds low; the other is to get the ball to come back near the side wall. To be sure the ball rebounds low, aim for an imaginary target low on the front wall — typically at about two feet off the floor (three feet for beginners).

   How close the ball comes to the side wall depends on where the ball strikes the front wall. The usual location is between one and two feet to one side of the center of the front wall. The more left or right of center the ball strikes the front wall, the more likely it is to rebound off the side wall before getting to the backcourt.

3. *Return trajectory.* The drive serve can rebound off the front wall either to the back corner, hitting the back wall

directly, or off the side wall before moving toward the back wall. Be sure you know *where you want the ball to end up*. Then adjust your target area accordingly.

Hints for Improvement

A strong drive serve should ricochet to the floor about five to seven feet behind the service box, close to the side wall. This assures that the ball is low and helps send it into the back corner.

Most Common Faults

The server hits the drive serve too high. This causes the ball to rebound high, giving your opponent the opportunity to play it off the back wall; or, the ball hits the side wall, then rebounds directly into the path of the opponent near centercourt.

Note: A drive serve that hits the side wall on the ricochet almost exactly at the juncture with the floor is extremely potent. This sends the ball low with short bounces. It becomes almost impossible to return because the opponent can't move up in time to get to it. This drive serve is commonly called an "ace serve."

Hints for Improvement

1. Accuracy is always more important than speed. Don't hit the ball so hard that you lose control.
2. All power serves should be kept as low as possible. During the serve, contact the ball below your shins.
3. The easiest shot for the receiver to return is a ball off the back wall. Don't hit the ball so hard that it rebounds into centercourt.
4. If you hit the serve too high and at too great an angle, the ball will rebound off the side wall into centercourt. Keep the ball low.
5. Mix your serves to both sides. Hit two out of three to your opponent's backhand.

Use boxes as targets while practicing serves.

• Drive Serve Drill

Accuracy is more important than power. Increase the power of the serve only when you are able to reach the expert scoring level (see "Scoring" below).

Place boxes on their sides in both corners and along the side walls about two feet behind the short service line.

Begin by hitting the drive serve from the center of the service box with your forehand. Observe where the ball hits the front wall and where it goes. If the ball hits one of the boxes, mark the front wall with a piece of tape where the ball made contact.

If you miss the box, alter the spot on the front wall where you hit the ball until you hit the box. Do this until you have four markers on the front wall that represent shots that hit the four boxes. In this way, you will eventually pinpoint the spots to hit on the front wall when executing your drive serves and be able to execute them strongly.

Once the markers are in place, hit ten serves at each marker. Give yourself one point every time you hit the box.

This drill should be repeated, hitting ten shots at each marker until you reach the intermediate score. When you accomplish this, move on to the advanced serves.

Scoring

0–1	Novice
2–3	Beginner
4–7	Intermediate
8–10	Expert

The Lob Serve

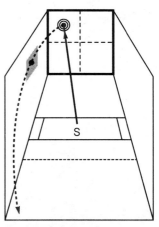

Target and path of high-lob serve.

The lob serve and the **garbage lob serve** are excellent ways to change the pace of the game, especially if your opponent is hitting kill shots off your drive serves.

The lob is a relatively slow high serve that skims the side wall and **dies** in the back corner. It is a difficult serve for both beginning and advanced players to return.

Hit the lob high on the front wall left of center. The ball arcs across the top of the court toward the side wall. (If the ball touches the ceiling, it is a fault.) The ball is slowed down by skimming the side wall and dies just before it reaches the back wall. An ideal lob dies in the very back corner of the court.

To hit the lob, use an upward motion with the racquet. Take care not to use so much force that the ball touches the ceiling.

The lob presents two great dangers. The first is that, if hit inaccurately, the ball fails to skim the side wall. This means that your opponent can return it easily in midair.

The second danger is that if you hit the ball with too much force, it rebounds far off the back wall. Your opponent can then play it off the back wall for a strong return.

If your opponent hits the ball hard, the lob provides you with an excellent change-up shot to throw your opponent off balance.

Lob Serve Technique Simply repeat hitting the lob serve at the front wall, then observe where it goes. You will improve by trying to get it to go as close to the side wall as possible and land in the corner. Put a box in the corner and see if you can drop the serves into the box. See the third level of the forehand drill for scoring information.

Garbage Lob Technique The garbage lob is a variation of the lob. It got its name because, to the inexperienced player, it looks like a weak serve that only a beginner would hit. Yet many professional racquetball players use the garbage lob.

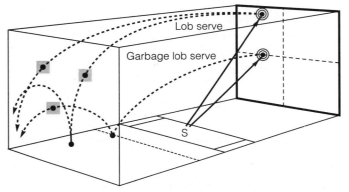

Comparative targets and paths of lob and garbage serves.

Hit the garbage and lob serves from about waist level or higher.

Hit the garbage lob serve a little harder than the lob and not quite so high. The ball drifts back, hitting the floor before it grazes the wall and dies in the back corner. The garbage lob serve should reach your opponent at about chest to shoulder height, making an offensive return almost impossible.

The difference between the lob and the garbage lob is that the latter has two arcs. The first lob of the garbage lob propels the ball off the front wall to the floor (just behind the service area) and near the side wall. From there, the ball rebounds high again, dying in the back corner.

The big advantage of the garbage lob is that it rebounds high in the back court (about chest to shoulder height) where your opponent tries to return it. This usually forces your opponent to hit a defensive ceiling shot.

Aim the garbage lob at the front wall about halfway up and just off the center. Hit this serve with medium force above waist level.

For both of these shots, your opponent must move to the back corner and hit the ball at chest height before it dies. This can be a difficult return for novices and even some advanced players. Advanced players understand how to handle lobs and garbage lob serves and can execute strong returns. However, if you hit these shots correctly, the return is usually a ceiling shot or some sort of defensive shot.

The real advantage of a **lob shot**, however, is that it changes the pace of a rally and often prevents your opponent from having an opportunity to ''kill'' the service ball. If you've been serving drives for a while, your opponent is conditioned to the speed of these serves. A lob can throw your opponent off balance and cause either a missed or a weak return. A well-timed lob can even cause an anxious overswing, resulting in a return that rebounds off the wall into center-court. At that point, you are in position to put the ball away.

Also, the lob forces your opponent to move to the back corner, which is a weak position. If you find that your opponent is killing many of your drive serves, immediately start serving lob and garbage lob serves.

The advantage of the lob serve is that it bounces high and forces your opponent to hit a defensive ceiling shot.

Most Common Faults

At higher levels of play, the lob and garbage lob should be change-ups, not ''bread and butter'' shots. The reverse might be true at the beginning level of play. Sometimes a server will unexpectedly serve a lob and score a point. Believing if it works once it will work again, the player might try it a second time.

That could be a bad idea, because a competent opponent is undoubtedly ready to answer another lob serve. However, if you can perfect the lob, it can and should be used more often as an offensive serve.

Hints for Improvement

The ball should just brush the wall, not touch it. The closer the ball is to the side wall, the more effective the serve.

Try to drop the ball into the box using the garbage and lob serves.

• Lob and Garbage Lob Drills

Place boxes in the backhand corner. Out of ten lob and garbage lob serves, see how many you can drop into the box. Use smaller boxes than those used in the drive serve drill.

Scoring

0–1	Novice
2–3	Beginner
4–7	Intermediate
8–10	Expert (Use the serve often)

If the ball brushes the side wall before going into the box, add one bonus point.

RETURNING THE SERVE

You must be ready and in position when you return the serve. Wait about two strides in front of the back wall and one-half step to the backhand side of the center of the court. (The backhand has a shorter reach than the forehand and you must compensate.) You need to be ready to return drives and lobs hit to either side of the court.

The receiver may not enter an area called the safety zone to return the serve until the ball bounces. The safety zone is the area between the short line and the receiving line. This

Position yourself about one foot toward your backhand side when returning a serve.

rule applies only on the serve. Violation of this rule gives the server a point.

Although you should watch the server and try to guess where the serve will be coming from, a competent server probably won't give much indication. A quick reaction and the ability to stretch to get to a ball may be what allows you to make the return.

Returning the Drive Serve

A good drive serve should normally be returned before it hits the back wall. Trying to hit it off the back wall may be difficult if it comes back and then dies on the floor.

As soon as you sense the server is hitting a drive serve, you should flex your knees. Then, as you determine which side the ball is coming from, turn toward that wall taking a large step (or two), and extend your racquet backward at the same time.

When hit properly, the drive serve comes so fast you must react before the ball reaches you. Thus, *your racquet should be halfway through the swing as you reach the proper position to hit the ball.*

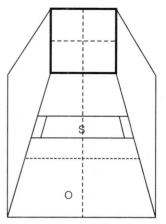

Position for return of serve: one to two feet toward backhand side.

Most Common Faults

Some players do not commit fully to returning the drive serve until it is too late. Remember, this is a powerful serve, and any hesitation will cause you to arrive too late to reach the ball. The ball will come in low, so start your swing early, anticipating a low contact point.

Hints for Improvement

The drive serve is the most common serve of intermediate to advanced players. Yet it is often hit inaccurately. Many times you won't need to go too far to get to it. If the ball makes contact with the wall, be ready for it to rebound toward you. A drive serve that is hit incorrectly can often be returned with a kill or pass shot. A well-hit drive serve is normally returned with a ceiling shot.

Returning the Lob and Garbage Lob Serves

The lob and garbage lob serves are high balls, which drift along the wall and fall into the back corner. You will probably have to hit the ball at shoulder height, requiring you to hit a defensive return. You have three options at this point — (1) ceiling return (the most common defense for either a well-placed lob or a garbage serve), (2) an around-the-walls shot (see Chapter 7: Shots for Advanced Players), or (3) if the ball is far enough from the side wall, a passing shot.

Most Common Faults

Because the lob and garbage serves look so easy, many players have difficulty believing that they should hit a defensive return. Additionally, they wait for a bounce off the back wall. However, by then it's too late, because a well-placed lob or garbage lob serve will die in the corner.

The second most common fault is trying to kill the ball. Because these serves are hit so softly, it is tempting to try to win the point outright. Most balls at shoulder height should be returned with a defensive shot.

Hints for Improvement

Lob and garbage lob serves are deceptive, but they usually give you time to respond. Try to hit the return immediately after the bounce or on the fly. The longer you wait, the lower the ball gets to the floor, making the return more difficult.

Basic Shots

Every racquetball player needs to perfect the basic shots. These are the shots that you execute over and over again, the shots that keep you in the game.

It's important to keep it simple at the beginning, to limit the number of different shots you try to use. Beginners need to master only three shots—the *kill*, the *pass*, and the *ceiling shot*. Perfect these three and you will become an expert in no time at all. In fact, ninety-five percent of all shots used in a game will be some form of these three shots.

As you advance, you will of course want to consider adding advanced shots to your repertoire. These are discussed in Part III of this book.

The two most important *offensive* shots are the pass and the kill. Because of the difficulty in executing the kill, beginners will find the pass easier to learn and perfect.

THE STRAIGHT KILL

If you followed the instructions and drills in Chapter 2, you should have perfected the kill by now. This shot can be executed from almost anywhere on the court, but for best results you should hit it from the middle of the court. Hit the ball very low, directly at the front wall. The ball hits the front wall just above the floor and bounces directly down, making a

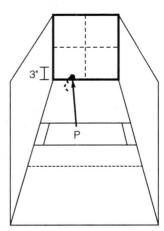

The straight kill can be hit anywhere on the front wall.

return next to impossible. A ball that hits the front wall and seems not to bounce but only rolls along the floor (a **roll-out**) is a perfect kill.

A straight kill can be hit with either the forehand or the backhand. However, it is important to hit the ball at a point about one foot off the ground. To do this, you must bend the hips and knees, flexing the entire body during the swing. You can gain power in the shot by quickly snapping your wrist at the moment the racquet meets the ball.

One benefit of trying to hit the direct kill from either side is that if you happen to hit the ball a little higher on the front wall, the shot will result in a good down-the-line pass.

Positioning to Hit the Ball

The ball is usually hit at one of three basic points: out of the air (1), immediately after it bounces (2) and begins its upward arc, or after the bounce and near the end of its downward arc (3). The best spot at which to strike the ball is at ankle level, after it has bounced, at the end of its downward arc. Not only will this give you more time to get into position, but it will also give you a better chance of making a kill. However, you should practice hitting balls at different heights.

Three places to contact the ball: (1) on the volley or fly, (2) on the half-volley, and (3) at the ideal place for good control (at ankle level).

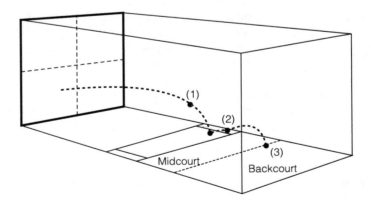

There are two opinions concerning the best position of the racquet face during ball contact: the face can be either flat (perpendicular to the ground) or open (tilted back slightly).

The advantage of the open-faced position is that it gives the ball underspin, causing it to bounce lower than a flat-stroked ball. The drawback of this method is that it may cause the ball to "float" and hit too high off the front wall. It is also not as powerful as the flat-faced position. What's more, those who favor the flat racquet face maintain that too much control is lost when the racquet is tilted. Most players hit kills with the flat-faced technique.

Beginning players should try both of these styles. Decide on one and practice it. Ball control and speed are developed with experience.

Most Common Faults

The ball is hit only a foot off the floor and the shot is aimed low on the front wall, so the trajectory causes the ball to skim just above the floor. Sometimes, however, in trying to place the ball low, you may hit it too low and make it touch the floor. On a service return, this scores a point for your opponent.

A second common fault is to attempt a direct kill when you aren't in proper position or when the ball is too high. The result is that the ball hits the front wall high, giving your opponent an excellent return opportunity.

Hints for Improvement

1. Don't hit this shot high on the front wall. The lower you let the ball drop before making contact, the better your chances for success.
2. Your chances for success increase the closer you are to midcourt. Don't hit this shot from the backcourt until you have mastered it from midcourt.

• Kill Shot Drill

Begin in midcourt. Drop the ball in front of you. Step forward, bending your hips and knees so that you contact the ball when it is only about a foot off the floor.

Aim for a spot low on the front wall. Stretch a piece of tape no more than a foot high across the front wall. Practice hitting the ball below the tape.

When you can hit the ball accurately in six out of twenty tries, move to the backcourt and try again using both forehand and backhand shots. Again, when you can hit six out of twenty shots below the tape, repeat the drills, tossing the ball off the side and back walls.

THE PINCH KILL

The pinch kill is an **offensive shot** that advanced players must master. A pinch kill is a shot that hits the side wall as close to the **crack** (the juncture between the side and front walls) as possible, then ricochets to the front wall and dies. It is a kill because, when properly executed, it is virtually impossible for your opponent to return the ball. In advanced play, it is one of the most important shots to have because it wins the point outright, which is the object of a rally.

The pinch kill is easiest to execute in the frontcourt. If your opponent knows you can use a pinch kill, he or she must work hard to make sure you don't have the opportunity.

For best results, the pinch kill should be hit from either frontcourt or the front of midcourt. Advanced players can hit the pinch kill from deeper in the court. The point is to hit the ball with enough force so that it first strikes the side wall (either the left or right wall, depending on your position and that of your opponent) very near the front wall. It then hits the front wall and dies in the frontcourt.

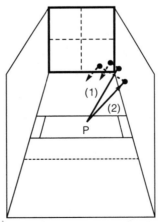

Pinch kills: (1) tight (best shot), and (2) wide.

The pinch kill is most effective when your opponent is behind you.

The best pinch kills are hit close to the crack and extremely low. Depending on your opponent's position, it is occasionally necessary to hit the pinch kill wider to get it farther out of your opponent's reach. This forces your opponent to the side of the court. However, hitting the pinch kill at a wide angle is difficult because extra power is needed to perfect the shot.

The pinch kill can also be hit off the front wall into the side wall, but this shot is used mostly by advanced players because it is difficult to execute. Try this variation after you have mastered the regular pinch kill.

Most Common Faults

Beginners have a tendency to hit the pinch kill *too hard* and *too high* off the side wall. The harder the shot is hit, the lower the spot at which it must contact the side wall near the front of the court. A hard shot hit high on the side wall drives the ball off the front wall with enough force to give it a good bounce into centercourt. The key to the pinch kill is accuracy. It must die in the frontcourt.

The biggest problem with this shot is that, if it is not executed perfectly, the ball ends up in the center and front portion of the court, which is the perfect position for your opponent to return a pinch kill, kill, or pass.

You can improve your chances of hitting a good pinch kill by doing two things:

1. Make contact with the ball as low to the ground as possible.
2. Aim for the crack. You will rarely hit it, and a slight miss will cause a perfect shot.

Hints for Improvement

If you don't have the pinch kill in your repertoire, your opponent will allow you to play the frontcourt and will drop back for better position. If you can hit a pinch kill, your opponent will want to keep you out of frontcourt or will be forced to be there with you. Use the pinch kill to score and the threat of it to keep your opponent from getting into a better position.

This is a shot you must master to be a good player. Practice the pinch kill for at least five minutes every time you are on the court.

● **Pinch Kill Shot Drills**

Place plastic tennis tubes in both corners. Start from mid-court, drop the ball, and hit ten forehands and ten backhands. Aim for either tube. When you are able to hit the tubes six out of twenty times, try tossing the ball off the side wall and hitting it after one bounce. After hitting the tube in six out of twenty tries, move to the backcourt and repeat the drill. Begin by dropping the ball, then tossing it off the walls.

HITTING TUBES

(From the backcourt, tossing the ball off the walls.)

Scoring (out of 20 shots):

0–2	Novice
3–5	Beginner
6–10	Intermediate
11+	Advanced

Begin in the **frontcourt** and drop the ball. Hit it at knee level or lower and hit a pinch kill. Then try tossing the ball off the side wall and hitting it after one bounce. As you improve, move deeper into the court, dropping the ball at first, then tossing it off the side walls. As you practice deeper in the court, you can toss the ball off the back wall and hit it after one bounce.

Aim for the tubes in the corners to perfect your pinch kill.

If you fail during your practice from frontcourt, return the bad pinch kill with a pass shot or defensive shot and rally with a few alternating shots before trying the pinch kill again. Practice the pinch kill with both forehand and backhand.

Put a plastic tennisball tube in the corner and try to hit it from backcourt. If you miss, you'll have a perfect pinch kill. If you hit it, the ball will be a perfect "crotch" kill.

The Two-Player Kill Shot

This is a set-up drill in which both players take specific positions and then execute a shot.

Both players should be in centercourt nearer one wall, one in front of the other. From a ready position, the player in back hits a down-the-line pass at the front wall. The player in front steps across to the wall and hits the ball while it is still in flight for a pinch kill, first to one corner, then to the other.

Exchange positions and try again.

THE PASS

The most obvious strategy of the game is to place the ball where your opponent isn't. If your opponent has to run to get the ball, it wears him or her down. It also means your opponent will not have as much time to set up the next shot, so you will probably get an easier return. The pass is an **offensive shot** that accomplishes these goals.

There are two pass shots—the down-the-line pass and the crosscourt pass. Because neither of these shots requires pinpoint accuracy, they are among the easiest shots to learn and use.

The Down-the-Line Pass

Hit this shot moderately low from one side of the court directly at the front wall. The ball rebounds along (but does not touch) the side wall.

Use this shot primarily when you are close to the side wall and your opponent is near centercourt or on the opposite side of the court from you. *Do not* hit the down-the-line

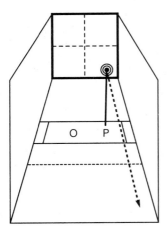

When you (P) are close to a side wall and your opponent (O) is near centercourt or on the opposite side of court, hit a down-the-line pass.

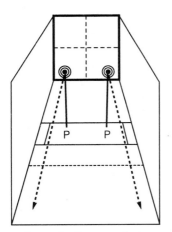

Down-the-line pass shots.

pass when your opponent is next to the wall. If your opponent is in front of you, both the down-the-line and crosscourt pass shots are effective.

Your goal is to hit the ball so that it strikes the front wall about three feet off the floor. The ball rebounds parallel to the side wall with enough power to carry it into the backcourt.

Because this shot is hit straight and rebounds straight back with little arc, you must hit the ball forcefully. However, do not hit it so forcefully that it reaches the back wall before bouncing on the floor.

Most Common Faults

In trying to make sure the opponent can't get to the ball, you may hit the down-the-line pass too hard. The ball may hit the front wall *too high* and have so much force left that it continues straight back to the back wall and rebounds into the perfect position for your opponent.

The point of the shot is to make the ball bounce in the backcourt, rendering a return difficult. Hitting it too hard or too high on the front wall defeats this purpose. The harder you hit the pass shot, the lower it must hit the front wall.

Hints for Improvement

In many cases, you cannot hit the ball accurately enough to make it rebound directly back. The down-the-line pass tends to cause the ball to hit the front wall and then career off the side wall on the way back. This means the ball ends up in centercourt—the perfect position for your opponent.

One way to avoid this is to aim your shot a little farther from the side wall than you normally would. Don't try to be perfect. Also, if possible, put a slight backspin on the ball. When it rebounds, it will then have a tendency to stay away from the wall.

The Crosscourt Pass

Aim the crosscourt pass at an angle from the center of the front wall. It should strike three to four feet above the floor. The ball will rebound at the same angle it is hit from (its trajectory will make a "V").

This shot is usually hit anywhere from midcourt to backcourt. The ball should be hit at waist height or below. It should be a power stroke, though not so powerful that the rebound off the back or side wall gives your opponent a good shot.

The crosscourt pass is most effective when your opponent is in the same half of the court as you, and is even more effective when your opponent is the closest one to the side wall. A crosscourt pass is ineffective when your opponent moves *farther away from you than centercourt*.

If your opponent is in front of you, both the crosscourt and the down-the-line passes are effective.

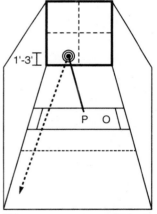

When your opponent (O) is closest to the side wall, hit *only* the crosscourt pass.

With your opponent in front of you, pass crosscourt or down the line.

In advanced play, the crosscourt pass has two additional goals: (1) It can be used to get the ball away from your opponent when both players are standing together on one side of the court; or (2) it can be used to move an opponent who is in front of you to the backcourt, allowing you to take possession of centercourt.

Most Common Faults

If the ball is hit too close to the side wall, it will not hit close to the center of the front wall and it will rebound off the side wall into the path of your opponent. It is important to hit the pass close to the center of the front wall to get the best angle for the rebound, but not too close to the side walls.

Hints for Improvement

As your play improves, you might want to hit the ball very slightly to the right or left of the center of the front wall, thereby slightly changing the angle of rebound. You only need to do this when you can accurately judge the rebound and you want the ball to move farther away from your opponent.

Don't hit the ball too high. The ball tends to gain height after it leaves the racquet anyhow, so a shot aimed lower usually ends up in the right spot.

Beginners should aim for a low kill while attempting the pass: The shot usually ends up being a perfect pass.

A Tip to Remember

Whether you should hit the crosscourt or down-the-line pass depends upon your opponent's position. There are only a few situations in which you should hit passing shots.

An easy rule is: You can hit the crosscourt pass as long as your opponent is relatively close to you.

Study these positions and practice them on the court. As you can see, the pass is used to get the ball *away from your opponent.* A common sense rule is: Don't hit the ball so it rebounds to your opponent. For example, you would never hit a down-the-line pass when your opponent is closer to the wall than you are.

Pass down the line (left) or crosscourt (right), but always *away* from your opponent.

Only a down-the-line pass would work here because your opponent is *farther away* from you than centercourt.

Wrong shot — — — — — — —

Correct shot - - - - - - - -

Passing Shot Selection Chart

1. Choose where you are,
2. choose the letter where your opponent is,
3. then choose the same letter to tell you what shot to hit.

You are:	Closest to the wall (in the midcourt area)	Centercourt	Backcourt	Frontcourt
Your opponent is:	a. close to you	a. in front of you	a. in front of you on the same half of the court	a. frontcourt, close to you
	b. near centercourt	b. behind you	b. in front of you on the opposite half of court	b. frontcourt, away from you
	c. further away from you than centercourt	c. on either side of you	c. backcourt with you	c. behind you in any position
Shot to hit:	a. crosscourt	a. usually down-the-line (if you hit crosscourt you'll probably hit your opponent)	a. crosscourt	a. kill or cross-court pass
	b. down-the-line or crosscourt	b. generally a kill	b. down-the-line	b. kill or down-the-line pass
	c. down-the-line	c. crosscourt away from your opponent	c. kill	c. kill

• Pass Shot Drills

The Repetitive Pass Drill

Begin with a down-the-line pass on the right side. Return it with another down-the-line pass on the right side. Continue for several shots, then hit a soft crosscourt pass. Move across the court and return with a down-the-line pass on the left side for several shots, then get back to the other side with another crosscourt pass. Repeat this drill until you can do this for several minutes without an error.

If you have a partner, alternate hitting down-the-line passes. See who misses first, then try the opposite side.

Also with a partner, stand at opposite sides near the backcourt. Hit crosscourt passes without stopping. When you can do this ten times without an error, change places. One partner should hit backhand passes while the other hits forehand passes.

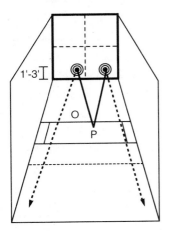

When your opponent is in front of you, hit either a down-the-line pass or a crosscourt pass.

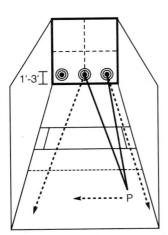

Individual pass drill. Hit several down-the-line passes, then hit a crosscourt pass. Move to the other side and hit several down-the-line passes, then hit a crosscourt pass. Repeat the drill.

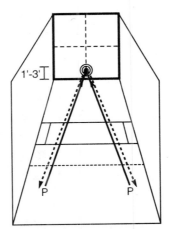

Repetitive crosscourt pass drill for two players.

• The Down-the-Line Pass Return Drill

Both players are ready at midcourt. One player hits a down-the-line pass. The other player races to the back corner to hit it.

Both players know what the shot will be. The element of surprise is that only the player who hits the shot knows which corner it will go to.

After the shot, retrieve the ball, set up, and try it again. After ten shots, exchange positions.

• The Crosscourt Pass Rally Drill

One player is just behind the short line, the other player is five or six paces behind him on the forehand side. The back player hits a forehand crosscourt shot.

The forward player must now drop back and retrieve the shot and the player in back moves up to centercourt.

Now the new back player hits a backhand crosscourt shot, forcing the new forward player to drop back to retrieve it. You are now in your original position.

After ten successful shots, switch positions so you can practice both the forehand and backhand crosscourt pass.

Advanced Serves and Serving Strategy

6

THE Z-SERVE

Once you've mastered the drive serve, you should be able to quickly learn the Z-serve. The Z is a strong serve. It is particularly effective as a change-up to the drive serve. After hitting a number of drive serves, your opponent can be taken off guard by a sudden Z-serve.

If you *serve from the center of the service box*, you can execute either a drive or a low Z-serve to either corner. This puts additional pressure on your opponent, since he or she won't know which to expect.

The Z-serve and the plain crosscourt serve (which will be discussed later) look identical. The difference between the two is in the power you exert. A ball hit extremely hard results in a Z-serve. A ball hit with less force results in a crosscourt serve. A Z-serve ricochets across the center of the court; a crosscourt serve bounces off the side wall, deep toward the back wall.

Hit the Z-serve into the front wall near the corner. It rebounds to the side wall, then ricochets across the court to the back wall and finally to the other side wall along a "Z"-shaped path. The ball must bounce on the floor *before* hitting the other side wall. One would expect that it would rebound to the back wall, but a strongly hit Z-serve rebounds *parallel* to the back wall because of the ball's spin. This unusual rebound can confuse an opponent.

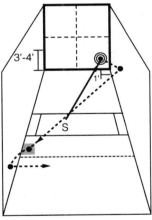

Z-serve target and path.

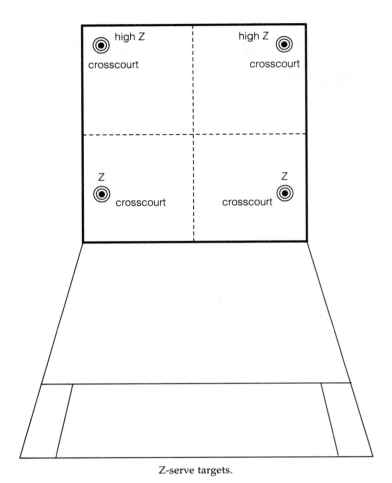

Z-serve targets.

The Z-serve is a highly effective shot because it forces your opponent to move rapidly into the corner or side wall for the return.

Hit the ball so that the ball strikes the front wall approximately two feet from the corner and three feet above the floor.

To get a better angle for this serve, stand one or two feet to the left or right of the service zone's center. Serve carefully, because the ball must strike the front wall before it strikes the side wall, or else it will be an "out."

Most Common Faults

Some players prefer to start the Z-serve while standing next to one or the other side wall. This may improve your chances of hitting a good Z-serve, but it may also tip off your opponent. In addition, it is almost impossible to hit a proper Z-serve to either side from one side of the service box.

The goal is to make it harder for your opponent, not easier, so stand in the center of the service box or slightly to the side of center.

Hints for Improvement

Hit the Z-serve hard. Since the Z-serve has to touch two walls before it heads to the opposite side wall, your opponent has an extra fraction of a second to respond. The harder the ball is hit, the less time there is to respond. A hard hit also means that the serve will have the spin necessary to produce the "Z-effect," in which the ball ends up rebounding parallel to the back wall.

The Crosscourt Serve

There are two variations to the Z-serve. The one we've briefly mentioned is the crosscourt serve, in which the ball travels in a path more resembling an "S" than a "Z." The only difference between the two serves is how hard you hit the ball. Hit a crosscourt serve at ½ to ¾ speed, which results in the ball rebounding toward the back wall without the Z effect. Practice hitting balls at different targets and at different speeds along the front wall.

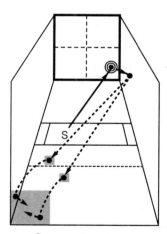

Crosscourt serves.

The High Z-Serve

The high Z-serve is simply a high crosscourt shot. The ball does not follow the Z-shaped path. Like the low Z-serve, hit this ball near the corner. The target area is just below the ceiling rather than just above the floor.

The goal of the high Z-serve is to produce an arcing ball that dies in the opposite back corner. (That is, it does not have the Z effect.) If your opponent is not expecting it, the

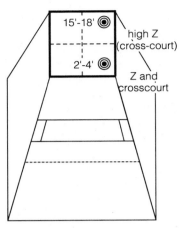

Targets for Z, crosscourt, and high Z (crosscourt) serves.

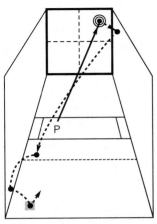

Target and path of high Z (crosscourt) serve.

high Z-serve can be an extremely difficult shot to return. To return this serve, your opponent must hit the ball while it is high in the air or scramble for it deep in the corner.

To get the high Z-serve right, you must hit the ball with an upward motion. However, take care not to use too much force, because this causes the ball to rebound off the ceiling (which is a fault).

• Z-Serve Drill

Place markers on the front wall so the ball produces the Z-effect deep in the backcourt. The closer the ball gets to the back wall, the better the serve.

Hit ten serves and award yourself one point for every ball that creates the Z-effect. Add one point to your score when the ball follows the Z-pattern between the short line and five feet from the back wall. Give yourself two points if it "Z's" five feet or closer to the back wall.

Scoring

0–3	Novice
4–6	Beginner
7–23	Intermediate
24–30	Expert

SERVING STRATEGY

Before serving, take a moment to clear your mind. If you are behind, or if your opponent has been intimidating you, you might approach the service timidly. Push this weak attitude aside. No matter how you have been playing before, the serve is your opportunity to score. A well-placed serve can give you an immediate point or result in a weak return, giving you an easy put-away. The serve can turn your fortunes around.

The biggest mistake committed by most players is putting the serve into play hastily, without considering the opponent's weaknesses. Use the serve as an *offensive weapon*, not just a means of beginning a rally.

Using Deception

When you prepare to serve, only *you* know where you want the ball to go. Your opponent eventually begins **anticipating** where you want the ball to go and compensates for it when preparing his or her return. Your advantage decreases in direct proportion to how soon you give away your intentions. The longer your opponent is unable to "read" your service, the less time he has to respond.

One method of keeping your opponent guessing is to develop a mixed bag of serves. It's a good idea to try out different serves on your opponent fairly early in the game.

Another method of keeping your opponent off balance is to use your opponent's anticipation to your advantage. Perhaps you stand a certain way or in a particular spot when you hit the ball to the left. After a few serves, your opponent will begin to anticipate your serve. If you're aware of this trait and have practiced hitting left when you're seemingly aiming to the right, try that. This sort of deception can throw your opponent off balance and win a point for you.

Confuse your opponent by not only changing serves but by making different serves look identical. When you change serves, change to one whose motion is similar to your previous serve. For example, you can follow a drive serve with a hard Z-serve. The motions for these two serves are similar. If you were to follow a drive serve with a lob, your opponent can immediately see the difference, giving him or her extra time to prepare the return. Particularly with drive serves and low Z-serves, deception is an essential part of advanced play.

Hints for Improvement

1. Relax. Remember that the serve is the only time in a game when you aren't rushed. Imagine how your serve will look and where it will go; think it through before serving. Take control.

2. Plan. Remember, you're on the offensive. Your goal is to put your opponent off balance.

3. Position yourself near the center of the service area. Avoid the side walls because this gives your opponent clues about your service plan and limits your options.

4. Be deceptive. If you can develop a similar swing for several serves, your opponent will not be able to anticipate your serve by your stance or swing.

5. Get on the offensive. The goal of the serve is to score a point. Don't think of it as just a way to begin a rally.

6. Use variety. Maybe you have one very good serve, but if you always use it, your opponent has an edge. Vary your shots to keep your opponent guessing.

7. Go for your opponent's weakness. In most cases, this is the backhand.

8. Always watch your opponent. After serving, move backward slightly, looking over your shoulder at your opponent. Watching your opponent will give you a hint as to what shot the return will be.

Watch your opponent. Move backward toward the side where you served the ball.

Returning the Z-Serve

Returning a well-hit Z-serve is rather difficult, primarily because it is disguised. The Z-serve and the plain crosscourt serve look identical. The only way to detect which serve is coming up is to observe how the ball is hit during the service motion. An extremely hard-hit ball results in a Z-serve. A ball hit lightly results in a crosscourt serve. Only after returning both these serves many times will you know which serve is coming.

A Z-serve ricochets into the center of the court. Therefore, you need not change your ready position or chase the ball. It will come to you. A crosscourt serve bounces off the side wall and flies deep toward the back wall.

If you cannot "read" these serves, you will constantly be out of position. If you are expecting a crosscourt serve, you will instinctively go to the back of the court. However, if your opponent hits a Z-serve, the ball will end up in the center of the midcourt area, putting you entirely out of position.

Most Common Faults

Beginning players often fail to recognize that when the Z-serve bounces off the side wall, it will have an unusual direction (caused by the spin of the ball).

Hints for Improvement

Stay in your ready position a fraction of a second longer on any crosscourt or Z-serve. Both of these serves normally end up in centercourt (where you should stand to return a serve). By hesitating just a moment, you are likely to be in position to return these serves.

The biggest mistake an inexperienced player makes is to move immediately toward the side wall where the ball is traveling. When the ball strikes the side wall, it rebounds sharply at a right angle into centercourt. The novice player is unable to make the return because he or she is either behind the ball or crashing into the wall.

SHOTS TO USE WHEN RETURNING SERVICE

In most cases, there are only four possible return shots. The shot you choose depends on the location of the ball and your opponent's position. They are listed here in order of importance. We'll discuss each separately.

1. a kill return
2. an aggressive return
3. a defensive return
4. just hit the ball

The Kill Return

It would be nice to hit a kill every time. However, you are usually least able to do so when your opponent is serving. Nevertheless, should the opportunity present itself, you should be ready. The best time to try a kill when returning a serve is when the server hits a poor serve that stays below your knees (usually the result of a poor drive serve).

You can attempt a kill any time you are well positioned to hit the ball. *You can hit one from either side at waist level or lower.*

The Aggressive Return

If you can't hit a kill return, your next best option is to hit an aggressive return. This means hitting the ball *hard*! You have at least two options open to you: (1) Hit a Z-shot. (2) Hit a pass either down the line or crosscourt. A good crosscourt or down-the-line pass can be as good as a kill shot and can win the point outright.

Defensive Returns

If you cannot win the point with a kill or an aggressive return, hit a return that puts your opponent in a bad position to win the point. This usually can be accomplished by hitting a defensive shot.

A defensive shot normally puts your opponent in the back of the court, where he or she has to hit a shot at shoulder height. The primary defensive shot is the ceiling ball. An alternative is the lob.

A lob is a change-up shot, which can also be an excellent defensive return. It can buy you some time and force your opponent to run out of centercourt and deep into backcourt.

Just Hit the Ball

If you are unable to execute a kill return, an aggressive return, or a defensive return, your final option is to just hit the ball to keep the rally going. This is strictly a defensive maneuver designed to recoup your position and your balance.

POSITION AFTER SERVING

As soon as you complete your service, you should begin to move diagonally back a few steps while still maintaining centercourt position. Be sure to position yourself slightly to the side where the ball is served. This protects you from a fast down-the-line pass.

Move to centercourt by shuffling back. This allows you to *move and watch your opponent and the ball at the same time.* Make sure you always watch your opponent. Many times, you can anticipate the next shot. As a precaution, protect your face by putting your racquet up to your face and looking through the strings.

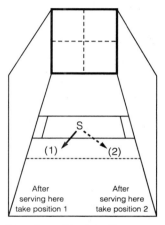

Server's positioning after serving. Move diagonally backward toward the ball.

After serving, move toward the side you served, watching the ball and your opponent.

POSITION AFTER RETURNING THE SERVE

The position you should take after you return a serve depends on what kind of return you hit. If you attempted a kill return, you should move to the center of the forward court, anticipating that the server might manage a return of your kill.

If you attempted an aggressive return, you should move to where you think your opponent will hit a return.

If you hit a ceiling shot, you should probably remain backcourt, waiting for your opponent to drop back and hit a return.

• Service and Return Drill

The purpose of this drill is to score on the service or the return. Both players set up in regular service and return positions. The server hits the ball. If the opponent is unable to make the return or hits an obviously weak return, the server gets the point.

If the opponent returns the service strongly with a good ceiling, pass, or kill shot, the opponent gets two points. The first to score ten points wins. Then the players should reverse positions.

There is no rally in this drill. After each service and return, set up again. This way, both players get to practice service and return.

Shots for Advanced Players

7

. . . .

Once you have mastered the three basic shots (see Chapter 5), you can move on to more advanced shots. These usually require greater accuracy and "touch" to execute properly.

THE Z-SHOT

The Z-shot is usually confusing to an opponent. However, if not executed properly, the chances are high that this shot will allow your opponent an easy opportunity to win the point. If perfected, though, the Z-shot can be most useful. Advanced players use it sparingly. Thus, when this shot is used, many players fail to react to the shot properly.

    The Z-shot is primarily a **defensive shot** hit much like the Z-serve described in Chapter 6.

    Aim the ball to hit high on the front wall, as close to the side wall as possible. The rebound takes the ball immediately into the side wall and then toward the backcourt. The ball then strikes the opposite side wall in the backcourt area on the fly. This is the only difference between the Z-shot and the Z-serve, which must bounce first before hitting the side wall.

    If hit with enough power, the Z-shot confuses inexperienced players. Instead of rebounding off the side wall toward the back wall, which would be the normal pathway of this shot, it rebounds across the court, parallel to the back

wall. Its full trajectory is described by a "Z." In games with beginning to intermediate players, this often results in a score, particularly if your opponent is out of position.

Most Common Faults

A good Z-shot is difficult to execute. You need accuracy to place the ball in the front corner, high on the front wall. The usual tendency is to hit it too low or too wide. In both cases, it will rebound into centercourt, setting up a perfect shot for your opponent. Also, the ball will only follow a Z-pattern if it is hit hard enough.

Path of a poor Z-shot not hit with enough power. A good Z-shot should hit close to the back wall and rebound *parallel* to the back wall.

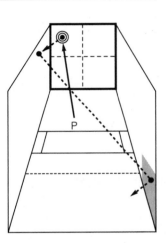

Paths of Z-shots: (1) hit too low on the front wall, rebounding to midcourt; (2) hit too weakly; and (3) hit properly.

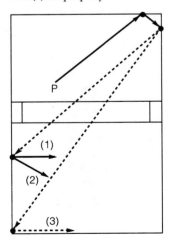

Hints for Improvement

The risk in hitting a Z-shot is that a bad one lands in centercourt, the exact place where you don't want it. A perfect Z-shot hits the side wall deep enough so that it bounces both parallel and close to the back wall. This keeps your opponent from getting the racquet between the ball and the wall to return the shot.

Practice hitting the Z-shot so that the ball strikes the rear wall as close to the back wall as possible. When you hit the ball so that it travels parallel to the back wall but only a foot or so away from it, it becomes extremely difficult for your opponent to return this shot. You should rarely use the Z-shot until you perfect it because, if executed improperly, it puts your opponent in a good position to win the point.

• Repetitive Z-Shot Drills

Stand in midcourt and begin by hitting the ball to the front wall with either your forehand or backhand stroke. (The contact point is usually shoulder height for the backhand and overhead for the forehand.) Anticipate where the return will be, and position yourself accurately for a return to the opposite front corner.

This takes practice. You can expect many missed balls at first, but this drill is very helpful in teaching you both where to place a Z-shot and where the rebound will go.

Practicing this shot and its return is best accomplished with two players. Stand in midcourt, each player on opposite sides. Begin by dropping the ball and hitting a forehand Z-shot. Your partner should return the shot with a backhand Z-shot. Repeat this until one of you makes an error. Change sides to work on both the backhand and the forehand shots.

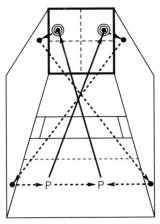

Repetitive two-player Z-ball drive.

THE CEILING SHOT

The ceiling shot is your bread-and-butter *defensive* shot. If you cannot hit a kill, if your opponent is overpowering you, or if you just want to slow the game down, use a ceiling shot. This shot prevents your opponent from executing a strong return.

Advanced players frequently have long rallies with numerous ceiling shots. This occurs when neither player can come up with a strong offensive return in response to a ceiling shot. Rather than chance a weak or inaccurate offensive return, each opponent returns the ceiling shot with another

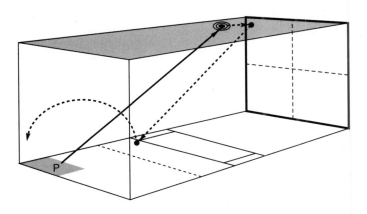

A *perfect* ceiling shot will just brush the back wall and die in the corner.

ceiling shot. A perfect ceiling shot drops almost parallel to the back wall or hits the back wall so low to the floor that a return shot is impossible.

To be effective, the ceiling shot requires great accuracy. Thus, you should practice this shot until you can get it to "hug" the side walls. Your opponent will not be able to easily handle this consistent accuracy.

The ceiling shot is hit either with the backhand or the overhead forehand strokes.

The Forehand Ceiling Stroke

The fundamentals for this stroke are similar to those for the forehand and backhand, with a few important differences:

Forehand ceiling shot.

1. On the backswing, bring the racquet back to a position behind your head. The bend at your elbow should be approximately ninety degrees. This motion is circular.

2. In the set position, the racquet is directly behind your back, with your elbow pointed toward the ceiling. The higher you raise your elbow, the lower the racquet will drop, allowing more arc and power in your swing.

3. The forward swing should be directed upward, with the elbow leading. Your entire body, including your arm, should be fully extended toward the ceiling. Make the wrist snap upward just before ball contact.

4. Meet the ball about a foot in front of your body with the racquet tilted back. This puts a slight underspin on the ball. The higher the point at which ball contact is made, the better your chances of hitting a powerful shot.

5. To exaggerate your follow-through, let your right arm touch your left hip. Trying to stop your stroke too early may result in damaged forearm muscles, or "racquetball-elbow."

6. Beginners should facilitate recovery by keeping their balance and anchoring their feet. Advanced players often take a step forward during their follow-through, ending the stroke with their feet crossed.

7. Remember, make the stroke a continuous motion. Contact should be made with the arm fully extended in front of you.

The Backhand Ceiling Shot

This stroke is perhaps one of the hardest to perfect. The form for the backhand ceiling stroke is similar to that for the regular backhand stroke, except contact is made near shoulder level, at approximately an arm's length away from the body. Because this stroke has to be hit powerfully, be sure that all your weight is transferred to your front foot during the upward swing. Upper body rotation is also important.

Follow through with the racquet across your body. The face of the racquet should be "open" or tilted backwards so that the ball angles upward toward the ceiling. The point of contact with the ball should be in *front* of your body, anywhere from chest to head height.

The most common ceiling shot goes directly to the ceiling about four feet in front of the front wall. From there it ricochets

Backhand ceiling shot.

down to the front wall and then to the floor. After it bounces on the floor, the ball arcs up and travels to the back wall.

Your opponent is most likely to be able to return your ceiling shot if he or she hits it before it reaches the back wall. However, by that time the ball is usually at shoulder height, making any offensive shot difficult. For this reason, many opponents hit the ball back to the ceiling.

When hitting the ceiling shot with the *backhand*, draw the racquet across the body. The ball angles upward because the face of the racquet is aimed at the ceiling and front wall.

When hitting the backhand ceiling shot, the point of contact is in front of your body, anywhere from chest to head height.

The Down-the-Line Ceiling Shot

The down-the-line ceiling shot is the most common ceiling shot. From the right side of the court, it is normally hit with the forehand; from the left side of the court, it is hit with the backhand. (Of course, most shots should be hit to the opponent's backhand, as it is usually a player's weaker shot.) The ball begins on the side of the court and returns after contacting the ceiling and front wall. The path of the return is down the line along the same side the ball was hit. If properly executed, the ball dies against the back wall.

The goal of the down-the-line ceiling shot is to get the ball *as close to the side wall as possible without touching it*. After bouncing on the floor, the ball skims along a fraction of an inch away from the side wall. This makes it very difficult for your opponent to hit the ball. An inexperienced opponent often rams the racquet into the wall trying to return this ball.

The Crosscourt Ceiling Shot

Hit this shot from one side of the court, angling toward the center of the ceiling. The crosscourt ceiling shot begins on the left side of the court and ends on the right (or vice versa). Use this shot when playing an opponent who has a dominant side different from yours.

Because the crosscourt ceiling shot cannot hug the wall like the down-the-line ceiling shot, it is easier for your opponent to return. Even so, it can force your opponent to move from one side of the court to the other, causing fatigue as well as surprise.

The standard ceiling shot *hits the ceiling first* and is easiest to hit. One variation on this occurs when the ball hits the *front wall first*. In this case, the ball hits the front wall about four feet below the ceiling, bounds upward to the ceiling, falls down to the floor, and after arcing upward, then dies at the back wall. Either method can be used as long as the end result is the same — that is, a difficult return for your opponent.

Most Common Faults

The most common error that novices make when hitting the ceiling shot is hitting the ball too soft or too hard. Also, going for the perfect shot too often causes a ball to ricochet off the side wall into the perfect position for an offensive return by your opponent.

Hitting the ceiling shot too hard puts your opponent in a position to kill the ball as it rebounds off the back wall far into the middle of the court. Hitting it too soft also puts the ball in a good position for an opponent's kill. Perfect "touch" is needed to execute this shot correctly.

Hints for Improvement

Use the ceiling shot

1.   when you want to change the tempo of the game,

2.   when your opponent is killing many of your returns, or

3.   when you are not in a perfect position to hit a kill or a pass.

Also hit the ceiling shot when your opponent has you out of position and you barely have enough time to get your racquet to the ball. Beware of trying to take a strong offensive shot after your opponent hits a well-placed ceiling shot. Many times the best return for a ceiling shot is another ceiling shot.

• Ceiling Shot Drills

Because the usual defense for a ceiling shot is another ceiling shot, just keep repeating the shot. First hit several down-the-line ceiling shots, then practice the shot crosscourt. Then move to the other side of the court and repeat the drill.

Try to hit this shot with a backspin, especially on the backhand. This helps beginners get the ball to bounce deeper into the backcourt.

Alternate hitting down-the-line ceiling shots with a partner, then practice on the opposite side.

Stand at opposite sides near the backcourt. Hit crosscourt ceiling shots without stopping (also with your partner). When you can do this ten times without an error, change places. One should hit backhand ceiling shots while the other hits forehand ceiling shots.

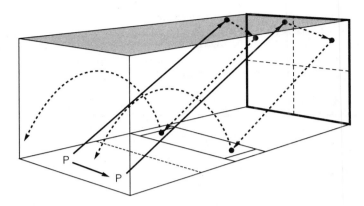

Individual ceiling shot drill. Hit several down-the-line ceiling shots; then hit a crosscourt ceiling shot. Move to the other side and hit several down-the-line ceiling shots; then hit a crosscourt ceiling shot. Repeat the drill.

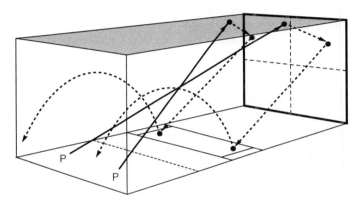

Repetitive crosscourt ceiling shot drill for two players.

• Ceiling Rally Drill

The purpose of this drill is to make a contest out of developing ceiling skills. You will learn two skills—how to hit good ceiling shots, and how to recognize when your opponent has hit a weak ceiling shot and take advantage of it.

Hit a kill on a weak ceiling-ball rally.

Both players begin hitting ceiling shots. Continue until one hits a weak shot, giving the other an opportunity to try for a kill.

If your partner returns the kill, end play and begin the ceiling rally again. If the kill is successful, the player who hit it gets a point.

Continue play until the winning player gets five points.

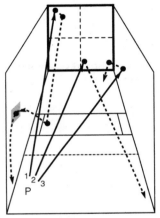

Overhead stroke options: (1) ceiling shot, (2) pass shot, and (3) overhead kill shot.

THE OVERHEAD STROKE

The overhead stroke should be used only when a player reaches the advanced level of play. Use the form described in this chapter for the ceiling stroke. The overhead stroke is performed in exactly the same manner as that for the ceiling shot, with one exception: The wrist snap at the point of contact is a *downward* and forward motion. By snapping your wrist over the top of the ball, you can hit the overhead stroke with considerable speed.

Use this stroke primarily in the backcourt when the ball is above shoulder height. The decision to use either the ceiling stroke or the overhead stroke depends on the type of return you want to make. Although the ceiling stroke is used only for the ceiling shot, you can use the overhead stroke to hit driving pass shots, lobs, kill shots, and even ceiling shots.

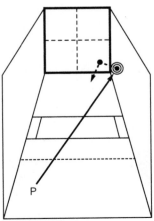

Path and target of the overhead kill.

THE OVERHEAD KILL SHOT

You should rarely use the overhead kill shot. This shot is an attempt to end the rally with one shot when you are deep in the backcourt (usually during an exchange of ceiling shots). The problem is that an overhead kill shot requires great accuracy and sometimes a bit of luck. If you miss, it is a sure point for your opponent. However, if your opponent knows that you aren't afraid to use this shot, it keeps your opponent guessing and off balance, anticipating your next shot.

Hit the ball down toward either front corner. The point is to hit the front or side wall close to the corner. The ball then bounces to the adjacent wall and dies before your opponent can get to it. The overhead kill shot is the same as the pinch kill shot, only hit from an overhead position deep in the backcourt.

Most Common Faults

This shot must be hit close to the crack of the wall. It is a high-risk shot. Beginning and intermediate players tend to use it too often. Use this shot rarely and only after you have perfected it. It's a "do or die" shot.

Hints for Improvement

Aim for the crack at the intersection of the front and side wall. You will almost never hit it, yet missing the crack slightly will cause a perfect overhead kill shot.

● **Overhead Kill Shot Drill**

Stand in the backcourt. Hit a bad ceiling shot that bounces away from the side wall. When the ball bounces high into the backcourt, hit an overhead kill shot to the front wall.

THE OVERHEAD PASS SHOT

Use this shot as an alternative shot during a ceiling rally. The overhead pass, overhead kill, and ceiling shots all look the same, which will keep your opponent guessing and confused during a rally.

The overhead pass shot is usually hit crosscourt from a position behind your opponent. When hitting the overhead pass shot, be sure to aim at a point four to five feet above the floor on the front wall. The goal is to catch your opponent off-guard, anticipating another ceiling ball. If your opponent is tiring, the overhead pass will find him or her unable to run to the opposite side of the court quickly to return the shot.

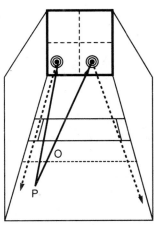

Path and target of the overhead pass shot.

● **Overhead Pass Shot Drills**

Stand in the backcourt. Hit a bad ceiling shot that bounces away from the side wall. When the ball bounces high in the backcourt, return it with an overhead pass. You can alternate practicing the overhead pass with the overhead kill because both use the ceiling shot as a set-up.

THE DROP (OR DROP KILL) SHOT

The drop shot is essentially a kill hit softly from frontcourt. Aim this shot low at the front wall. Hit it with a "pushing" motion rather than a wrist snap to eliminate any bounce on the rebound. The point is to have just enough power for the ball to touch the front wall, drop to the floor, and die. Your opponent must be in *backcourt* when you execute this shot. To return it, your opponent has to dash madly from the backcourt to the front wall, usually an impossible feat if the shot is executed and disguised properly.

Most Common Faults

Beginning players often do not know where their opponent is on the court. The task of watching both the ball and the opponent can be very difficult from the frontcourt. It requires that you constantly check to see where your opponent has moved. Hitting a down-the-line pass on the right side works only if your opponent is still on the left. If your opponent moved to the right, you will probably lose the point. Similarly, hitting a drop shot can have a bad outcome when you think your opponent is in the backcourt but he or she has actually moved up. Knowing where your opponent is at all times is one key to advanced play.

• Drop Shot Drill

You need two players for this drill. Have one player set up in the frontcourt and the other set up in the backcourt. The back player hits a shot that rebounds off the front wall toward the front player. As it rebounds, the front player executes a drop shot on the fly to the bottom of the front wall.

A few minutes of this drill practiced regularly over time can produce good results.

THE AROUND-THE-WALLS SHOT

The **around-the-walls** shot is another defensive shot that can be used as an alternative to a ceiling or a Z-shot. This shot can be difficult to return even for an experienced player, but it's not the kind of shot you'd want to use repeatedly. Occasionally, though, it can be used to keep your opponent off balance.

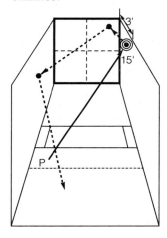

Target and path of the around-the-walls shot.

Hit this shot with either the forehand or the backhand high into the side wall near the front of the court (in contrast, the "Z" hits the front wall first). The ball bounces to the front wall and then the opposite side wall and, if executed properly, heads downward toward the backcourt. This angle makes it difficult to return. The around-the-walls shot hits high on three walls, causing the ball to lose most of its momentum and then drop fast toward the backcourt.

Most Common Faults

The most common problem that beginners have with this shot is that they inadvertently hit the ceiling. This sends the ball to centercourt, setting up a perfect return for your opponent.

This shot is not hard to hit, but it does require excellent "touch." It is important to remember that the ball should strike high on the first side wall so that it remains high when bouncing to the front wall and the opposite side wall. The best trajectory for this shot is about three feet from the front wall and about five feet down from the ceiling.

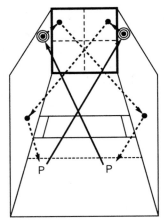

Repetitive around-the-walls shot drill for two players.

Hints for Improvement

Use the around-the-walls shot sparingly. A strong opponent might be able to catch it on the fly and execute a kill shot to the front wall.

• Repetitive Around-the-Walls Drill

Begin in midcourt. First hit the ball to the right wall. Observe the trajectory and be in position for a return. Then hit the return to the left wall. Alternating walls in this fashion gives you practice in both hitting the shot and anticipating the return.

Two players can hit alternating around-the-walls shots. Stand opposite each other in the backcourt and hit the shot to the opposite corner. It should rebound to the other player, who then returns it to you. Practice both the forehand and the backhand shots.

• Multidrills for Alternating Shots

Once you have a fair mastery of these shots, try to mix them up. As mentioned in Chapter 5, ninety-five percent of the game requires only the three basic shots. Advanced shots are the icing on the cake and should be used as a surprise tactic. This keeps your opponent off balance.

Strategies During a Rally

· · · · · · · ·

8

Once the ball has been served and returned, you are in a rally. In today's play there are two kinds of rallies:

- *The Offensive Rally.* The players try to execute a kill shot every time the opportunity presents itself.
- *The Defensive Rally.* The players try not to give their opponents a chance to kill the ball while forcing the opponents into a weak return, thereby enabling them to go for the kill.

Although a good, consistent, offensive player can overpower a weaker opponent, a player who mixes defensive shots, positioning, sound strategy, and offensive shots can easily equal or better a more powerful opponent. The reason for this is simply that constantly going for the kill requires pinpoint accuracy from all areas of the court, something that very few of us can master.

Although going for the kill can be an important goal, *sustaining* a rally until you have a *good opportunity* for a kill is as important a strategy as hitting the kill.

CONTROLLING THE CENTERCOURT POSITION

The person who controls centercourt usually wins the game. This does not mean you must be in centercourt at all times. You must move to different positions to return shots and to execute different shots. But an important goal is to *return to centercourt position whenever possible.*

You can maintain centercourt position through intelligent shot selection. By picking and choosing your shots, you can force your opponent into the backcourt, thus maintaining control of centercourt yourself.

SHOT SELECTION

Here are three general strategies to remember:

1. Avoid shots in which the ball ends up in centercourt (except for kill). Try for shots that end up in the backcourt.
2. Try to keep your shots low.
3. Hit the ball away from your opponent.

FINDING YOUR OPPONENT'S WEAKNESS

In addition to selecting shots for position, it is also important to tailor your shots to your opponent.

At the beginning of play, test your opponent for weak areas by diversifying your shots. This is usually easy for beginning players because most shots tend to be of about equal quality, with the backhand being particularly vulnerable.

However, developing a strategy is more difficult for intermediate and advanced players because there might be one or two shots that an advanced player hits consistently well. *Once you recognize your opponent's strengths, continue to hit the ball to his weaknesses.*

Hints for Improvement

Hit your shots to the backhand most of the time. Your opponent probably has a weaker backhand because the backhand is normally a more difficult stroke to master. However, be on the alert for players who have strong backhands and weak forehands. (This is usually the case only at advanced levels of play.)

PLAYING TO YOUR OPPONENT'S WEAKNESS

Once you've identified your opponent's weakness (either a weak stroke, a weak return of a particular shot, or both), aim for it. However, you should not play to your opponent's weakness by exposing your own weakness.

Go with your strengths whenever possible. Ideally, hit your stronger shots to your opponent's weaknesses.

Hints for Improvement

For beginning players, hitting any shot accurately is difficult. Therefore, beginning players should concentrate on hitting well-placed shots away from the opponent and to the backhand, then returning to centercourt.

Advanced players are usually very accurate shot-makers. For these players the focus of the game changes from placing shots well to selecting just the right shot for the moment.

THE PLAN OF ATTACK (BEGINNING STRATEGY)

As a beginner, your plan is just to hit the ball and keep it in play. However, the better you become, the more important it is to have a plan of attack thought out before the game. Perhaps your plan will be to test your opponent first and then concentrate on your opponent's weak areas. As long as your game plan seems to be working reasonably well, stick with it.

However, sometimes in the course of the game you may find yourself falling behind in spite of your game plan. Adaptability is now the key to your success.

Being adaptable means being willing to change your game plan when it isn't working. Perhaps your opponent has guessed what you are doing and is prepared to defend against it. If so, a change-up shot could throw your opponent off. Instead of trying to make aggressive kills and pass shots, perhaps a defensive ceiling and Z-shot game will work. Changing the pattern of your shots may produce positive results as well. Instead of overpowering your opponent, an occasional around-the-walls or lob shot could throw him or her off balance. Remember, *strategy is only possible after you have mastered the strokes* and can place your shots consistently and accurately.

Rules to Remember

Whatever your game, here are four more rules that you should find helpful:

1. *Don't just try to play a game of power.* Accurate passing shots and change-ups can force your opponent into weak returns that you can take advantage of.
2. *Go for a kill shot whenever the opportunity exists.* Don't try for a kill shot unless your likelihood of making it is at least seventy-five percent.
3. *Use speed and change-ups to throw your opponent off.*
4. *Aim for where your opponent isn't.* If he's in the backcourt, try a frontcourt kill shot. If he's in the frontcourt, try a pass to the backcourt.

ADVANCED STRATEGY

When you are consistently placing your shots, you must be concerned with hitting the best shot in response to your opponent's position.

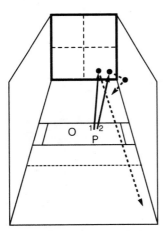

With both opponent and player in midcourt, hit (1) pass shots or (2) kill shots. Hit these shots to either side.

Strategy for Midcourt Rallies

When rallying in midcourt, you are typically in the center; your opponent may be next to you or in front of or behind you. When you command midcourt position, you are at your strongest and your play should reflect this.

When in midcourt, you have an opportunity to play aggressive racquetball. Whether your opponent is in front of or behind you, you have the controlling position. You should pick your shots with an eye toward scoring. From midcourt, it's important to use every chance you get to either go for a kill or give your opponent a difficult return. Here are four strategies to employ when you are in midcourt:

1. Hit the ball *hard* from midcourt. This gives your opponent little time to respond to your shot.

2. When your opponent is also hitting in midcourt, you can expect him or her to try down-the-line and crosscourt passes. Your goal should be to return these forcefully, either with a down-the-line pass or with a kill shot (diagram at left). When you are in this position, it is to your advantage to keep the ball low and moving fast. Quick exchanges occur here, and you must react instinctively by hitting kills and passes with power!

3. If your opponent moves to the frontcourt while you are in midcourt, you must change your strategy. *Kill shots should be avoided*. Your opponent will be in a perfect position to return them with another kill that you would have trouble reaching.

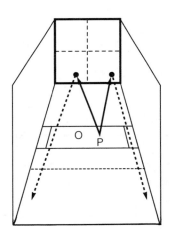

Hit passes with the opponent in front and player behind in midcourt.

As soon as your opponent moves in front of you, the pass shot becomes a good aggressive play. Your opponent shouldn't be able to react fast enough to cut it off (assuming you hit it away from him or her). Then your opponent will be forced to race for the backcourt in what will probably be a vain attempt to retrieve the shot. A pass shot could score under these circumstances.

4. Whenever your opponent is behind you, especially in the backcourt, you should immediately go for the kill. With your opponent in the backcourt, your chances of

Hit kill shots with the opponent behind the player.

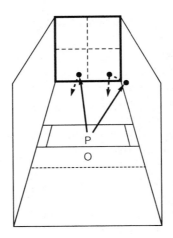

scoring on a kill shot are excellent. Even if you hit the kill shot too high, your opponent has a long way to run to get to the ball.

Don't hit any pass shots when your opponent is in the backcourt. You can't pass your opponent if he or she is in the backcourt. If you expect to execute an effective pass shot, your opponent should be no further back than midcourt. If your opponent is in the backcourt, a pass will go right to him or her. You want to make your opponent run to hit a shot. A good player will kill most balls when they are allowed to stand still and set up.

On the other hand, many good players anticipate certain shots and try to run to the spot where they think you will hit the ball. This happens frequently when your opponent is behind you and you correctly go for a kill. Knowing this is your best shot in this situation, your opponent will run to the frontcourt just as you are hitting the ball.

If your kill is ineffective because your opponent is rushing forward and "picking it up," then hitting a pass is a perfect response.

Remember that centercourt (or midcourt) is the best position during a rally. Try to stay out of other areas of the court, if possible.

WHEN YOU CANNOT CONTROL CENTERCOURT

If you find yourself in the front- or backcourt, the following general rules apply:

Frontcourt

If you find yourself in frontcourt, your choice of shots depends on your opponent's location.

1. Whenever you are in frontcourt and your opponent is behind you, *go for the pinch kill shot*. However, the closer your opponent is to you, the more opportunity arises to use the pass. Remember, the kill is a bread-and-butter shot when your opponent is behind you.

2. Whenever your opponent is beside or in front of you and you are in front- to centercourt, *go for a pass shot*. This is a sure-win situation for you *if* you can execute a pass to the back wall. There's little chance your opponent can move quickly enough to the backcourt to return the ball.

Most Common Faults

Most beginning and some intermediate players suddenly see the opportunity to score but hit the pass shot too hard. It goes deep to the back, bounces off the back wall, and falls in position to be returned by your opponent.

Hints for Improvement

Hit all passing shots as hard as you can and about a foot off the floor. If you miss, you're likely to hit a kill.

Try for a down-the-line pass so that you are between the ball and your opponent. This is not the same as "blocking" your opponent from the shot. It simply means that he or she has the farthest distance to go to return it.

RALLY STRATEGY FOR THE BACKCOURT

With both players in the backcourt, your backcourt shots usually depend on the shot your opponent hits rather than his position. Both players usually end up in the backcourt after a ceiling-ball rally. If your opponent hits a weak ceiling or defensive shot with the ball rebounding to centercourt, go for a kill.

However, if your opponent hits a good defensive shot, don't lose your patience. Return a well-placed defensive shot with a well-placed defensive shot. Wait for the opportunity to win the point. Don't create an opportunity for your opponent to win the point. *Rallying from the backcourt takes patience and accuracy.*

Experienced players are aggressive in the backcourt only when the opportunity presents itself. Your skill level must be very high to end the rally. There's a time for good aggressive shots, but not when you're out of position and your opponent is in a good position.

Hints for Improvement

To be safe, be defensive. Force your opponent back with you. Although this may not give you an advantage, at least you'll be on an even footing. Wait for your opponent to make a mistake in positioning. Once you can gain a good position and good footing, "go for it."

The Direct Kill from the Backcourt

Many intermediate and even beginning players have a good kill shot from front- and midcourt, but often do not have a strong backcourt kill. Backcourt kills are extremely difficult to execute and usually occur only at an advanced level of play. The ball is hit low and must travel the entire distance of the court before it strikes the front wall very close to the floor. This shot is seldom executed successfully and should be used only as your game improves.

However, you can be sure that as soon as your opponent discovers you don't have a backcourt kill, your opponent will take to the ceiling, force you back, and then score with his or her own backcourt kill.

A good backcourt kill can be developed. It's not a shot with a high rate of successful execution, so you shouldn't use it often. But just letting your opponent know you have it will keep your opponent from forcing you into rallying from the backcourt and then executing the backcourt kill to beat you.

The reverse is also true. If you develop a good backcourt kill and notice your opponent has trouble with this shot, hit defensive shots and ceiling balls until your opponent makes a mistake, and then kill the ball.

Most Common Faults

When the opportunity presents itself, many intermediate and advanced players go for the kill and use the ceiling shot to both keep the opponent off balance and prevent him or her from returning a kill. Beginners tend to forget the great advantage of the ceiling shot—it drives your opponent back.

The goal of a ceiling shot, though defensive in nature, is to get either a better position or a better shot opportunity from your opponent. It is a highly successful shot when hit from the backcourt.

PLAYING OFF THE BACK WALL

The ability to play off the back wall is vital to a player at any level. Back-wall play is probably the most difficult thing for a beginner to learn. If you hope to be competitive and play well, you should master back-wall play.

Playing off the back wall is a strong approach. Typically, players will hit aggressive shots such as kills or passes from this position. In a long rally, many shots may be played off the back wall.

There are two methods of playing off the back wall. The first is to wait for the ball as it comes off the wall and hit it. This is the standard shot.

The other method is to hit the ball *back* into the wall. Use this shot only when the ball has passed you and there is no chance to get it before it bounces twice. Advanced players use this shot only in desperation, but beginners tend to use it regularly.

Taking the Ball off the Back Wall

Wait until the ball hits the back wall and begins to travel forward. Get into position and don't rush the shot. The ball is usually low, at the optimum position for a forehand or backhand drive. If you position yourself properly, you can hit the ball forcefully. The shot you hit is usually an aggressive one—a kill or a pass.

The key to making this shot is being in proper position. When you hit the ball, you should be ready with your feet "set and planted." Be patient and make contact with the ball as low as possible, preferably at knee to ankle level.

If you hit the ball when it is behind you, the angle of your racquet will deflect it to the side wall and your shot will be wasted. If you hit the ball when it has passed you, it will be a weak shot with possibly the same result.

Getting into Proper Position If you are in centercourt or any forward position, you *must* drop back quickly because the ball rapidly loses momentum once it hits the back wall. To hit a good shot coming off the back wall, position yourself within a few feet of the wall.

Beginners usually attempt to drop back by turning and sprinting for the back wall. While doing this, they often lose sight of the ball and cannot determine its relative speed. They might get back in time, but they usually either lose the shot while trying to locate the ball, or the ball rebounds hard off the back wall and travels back to midcourt while the beginner is standing in backcourt trying to hit it.

You must *both* drop back *and* watch the ball by turning to face the side wall. You can now watch the ball and position yourself better near the back wall as the ball comes off it. This might sound like a difficult feat, but with practice it comes naturally.

Once you've determined that you'll need to play the ball off the back wall, use any footing you find comfortable to keep yourself facing the side wall and moving toward the back with the ball. For most players, this amounts to extending the foot nearest the back wall, then bringing the other foot up to it and repeating this simple "sideways shuffle." Avoid trying to place one foot over the other, as in normal running. This will only cause you to trip.

Once you're close to the back wall, judge where you want to make contact with the ball. The most common method of doing this is to move back, set up, and then hit the ball. As soon as the ball rebounds, judge its position and take the shot.

Another method is to move all the way to the back wall, watching the ball and judging its trajectory with the racquet back in a ready position. Then reverse direction, moving forward just as the ball rebounds, and hit it while you are in a "sliding" forward motion. Although this adds power to the shot, it requires greater skill. Use this method when the ball is hit very hard and rebounds off the back wall far into the midcourt area.

Most Common Faults

The most common mistake beginning players make is that they don't watch the ball continuously. Taking your eyes off the ball even for an instant causes confusion when you try to find it and it then becomes very difficult to hit.

Players also make the mistake of not dropping back far enough. The ball then bounces behind them, making a return impossible. You must position yourself between the wall and the ball. One way of knowing when you're deep enough is to make physical contact with the back wall with an outstretched hand or the racquet.

Hints for Improvement

Hit the ball when it is low. As it rebounds off the back wall, it begins to drop. Your most powerful shots come at about calf level. Take the ball there.

HITTING THE BALL INTO THE BACK WALL

This is a desperation shot. Use it only when you can't execute any other shot.

Make this shot by hitting the ball into the back wall after it rebounds. The ball must travel the entire length of the

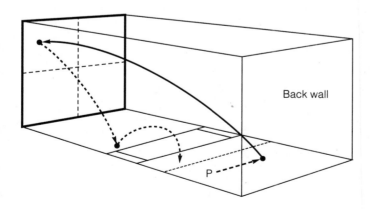

Ball into the back wall shot.

Back wall

P

court and touch the front wall before it hits the floor. If the ball is to strike the front wall, you must hit it with maximum force. Even so, so much energy is spent in striking the back wall at close range that the ball arcs forward, hitting the front wall with little force. This sets up an easy kill for an experienced opponent. Make sure you hit the ball with an upward motion; otherwise you may get the ball right back in your face.

● Back Wall Drills

Stand in the backcourt close to the back wall. While standing sideways, toss the ball off the back wall and try to hit it before it bounces. When you perfect this, hit the ball hard and high on the front wall so it hits the back wall after bouncing on the floor. Practice shuffling back and setting up to hit the ball before it hits the floor.

Doubles and Cutthroat

9

DOUBLES

Doubles play and cutthroat play are fun. Although there are more people on the court in these types of play, which may increase the chance of an accident, doubles and cutthroat can be challenging and enjoyable. Even if you prefer singles play, playing doubles occasionally can improve your singles game.

Players of different ages and abilities can enjoy playing together in doubles. Doubles can be a less strenuous and more relaxed and sociable game; however, it requires greater concentration and strategy to win.

Doubles requires the use of more angles on pass and kill shots and greater accuracy to win points. In singles, front-wall passes and kill shots are often good enough to win a point. However, in doubles, there are two people to be passed, and therefore, you have to use the angles to get the ball around the players.

Good doubles is played with a flowing motion, as in dancing. In a ballet or waltz, the motion is continuous but fluid and smooth. In doubles play, the four players move in and out of centercourt continuously, trying to gain an offensive advantage. Even more so than with singles, the team that wins in doubles is the one best able to cover centercourt.

Poor doubles play looks like the "Three Stooges," with lots of random, jerky movement and plenty of collisions and erratic shots.

Positioning

To avoid running into each other and for best court coverage, doubles teams use one of two positions — **right/left** or **side-by-side**, and **front/back** or **"I" formation**.

Right/left   The right/left method (also called side-by-side) divides the court down the middle with an invisible line. One player takes the right side, the other the left.

It's not quite that simple, however. In determining which side to take, consideration should be given to (1) which player has the better backhand (that player should take the left side if both players are right-handed), (2) whether one partner is left-handed and the other right-handed, and (3) who is the stronger player.

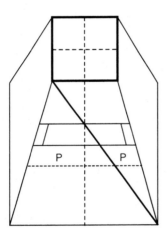

Doubles right/left position.

Depending on the make-up of the team, the court may actually be divided *not quite* down the middle. The stronger player should play one side *and* most of the center, while the weaker player should play the other side.

Front/back   In the front/back method, one player stands in front of another. This formation is particularly useful if one player has quick reactions and is adept at kill shots and the other is an excellent backcourt player.

The problem with the front/back formation is that strong down-the-line shots can get by both players.

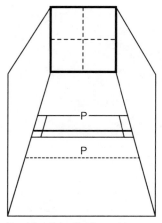

Doubles front/back position.

Doubles front/back position.

Safety

With four players on the court, safety becomes a concern. It can be dangerous when players crash or bump into each other and when racquets swing close to a player. To make a game safer, players should let their partner know where they are. Players should also "claim" or "call" shots to help avoid collisions. Players must also watch the ball at all times, not only to be prepared to hit it when it comes to them, but also to avoid being hit by the ball when it is hit by someone else. Keep your racquet up at all times to protect your face if you can't get out of the path of the ball.

Serving

At the beginning of each game in doubles, each side determines the order of service that must be followed throughout the game. When the first server is out or loses the first time up, the team loses the serve, which is called a **sideout**. Thereafter, both players on each side serve until each player loses his or her serve. (One player losing a serve is called a **handout**.)

On each serve, the server's partner stands erect with his or her back to the side wall and both feet on the floor within the service box. The partner must stand in the box from the moment the server begins the serving motion until the served ball passes the short line. Violations are called "foot faults."

There is no rule requiring the server to serve to a specific opponent; therefore, you can serve to either one. Generally you will not win the point on your serve in doubles, so serve the ball deep in the backcourt to keep the receivers back. This allows the serving team to control centercourt.

A lob or Z-serve will keep the receivers from hitting an offensive return, but will usually start a ceiling-ball rally. A drive serve is a little riskier because if it is not hit properly, it will be returned offensively with a kill or pass.

Mix your serves and occasionally serve to the other opponent. Of course you want to serve to the weaker receiver, but mixing your serves will keep your opponents guessing.

Basic Strategy

Because there are two opponents in doubles, it is far more difficult to execute a quick kill. Therefore, doubles requires a defensive strategy of waiting until the opportunity arises to go for the kill. Hit a kill shot only when you have a perfect set-up or the opposing team is out of position. If your opponents are in good position, a missed kill is easier to return than it is in singles play.

Patience is rewarded in doubles. Covering for your partner is also an essential element. When one partner goes for a shot, the other may be temporarily forced to abandon a portion of centercourt. Leaving that vital area unattended invites disaster. Therefore, some partners agree that, when one partner goes for the ball, the other will cover centercourt.

As soon as the ball is hit, the partners return to either the right/left or front/back position.

There are six rules that help a doubles team dominate centercourt and win the game:

1. Know which is the stronger partner. If possible, let the stronger player on your team take the most difficult shots and all shots in the center of the court.

2. Identify the weaker player on the opposing team and aim all your shots at that person. If one opponent is playing particularly well, direct your shots away from that player.

   Sometimes a team will have a weak side. Perhaps both players are right-handed and both have weak backhands. Direct shots to their backhand whenever possible.

3. Go to different positions. Don't bunch up. If your partner is hitting the ball, you should go to centercourt or to another advantageous position. You should avoid situations in which you both chase the ball.

4. Work on team play. You must watch not only the ball and your opponents but your partner as well. If you see your partner is out of position, choose a ceiling shot to give your partner the opportunity to get back into position.

5. Be patient. Use defensive shots. Sometimes it is possible to confuse opponents who are playing in the right/left position by sending a shot down the middle.

   When you see an opening, hit a decisive kill. Pinch kills are often the most effective shots in doubles. But be sure you are in front of both your opponents.

6. Try to keep your opponents off-balance. Use pass shots and around-the-walls shots to confuse them.

Doubles can be difficult to learn for beginners. The confusion of four inexperienced players on one court makes safety a primary consideration. Beginners should master cutthroat before attempting to play doubles.

CUTTHROAT

Cutthroat is played in most classes. The game is similar to doubles, but it is played with only three people. There are three types of cutthroat: (1) rotation, (2) stand-out, and (3) two against one.

Rotation

This type of cutthroat is the one most commonly played. As its name implies, this form of cutthroat's players rotate the serve. A rotation (usually clockwise) is established before play begins. When the server loses the rally, the next player in rotation becomes the new server. The previous server takes over the vacant spot and the players move into new positions. The server always plays against two opponents.

Rotation can also be played with four people; however, the fourth player stands out and rotates in.

Stand-out

In stand-out cutthroat, players play the rallies in the standard singles format, with the third player "standing out" (usually against the back wall). The loser of a rally stands out, while the previous stand-out player steps up to receive the serve.

Two Against One

This form of cutthroat is the most challenging. Two players team up against the third and play until one side accumulates eleven points. After each game, a new team is formed. The player with the highest point total after three games is the winner.

Cutthroat: two against one.

Strategy for Cutthroat

As you can imagine, in rotation and two-against-one it is difficult for the server to score and easy for the opponents to win the rally. As the server, apply the six rules mentioned earlier and aim most of your shots at the weaker player. If both opponents gain centercourt, a high side-wall pass shot is a good offensive shot. This shot is just like the regular pass, but it is hit five to six feet high on the front wall and closer to the side wall. The ball will ricochet from about four to five feet up the side wall behind the doubles team.

As in doubles play, the receiving team can make the server run wildly over the entire court by hitting passing shots.

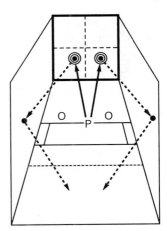

The high side-wall pass is a good shot for cutthroat.

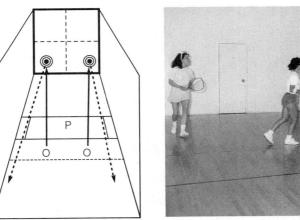

Passing shots in cutthroat keep the server running around the court.

10

Fitness for Racquetball

Racquetball is an exciting and physically demanding sport. You can improve your skill as a player, help prevent injuries, and increase your overall level of fitness by making racquetball part of a complete exercise program.

COMPONENTS OF PHYSICAL FITNESS

Physical fitness is the ability to adapt to the demands and stresses of physical effort. It has five basic health-related components:

- **Cardiorespiratory endurance (CRE):** The ability to do moderately strenuous activity over an extended period of time. CRE is a measure of how well your heart and lungs supply your body's increased need for oxygen during sustained physical effort.
- **Muscular strength:** The ability to exert maximum force in a single exertion. Lifting a heavy weight or taking a step up the side of a mountain is a measure of muscular strength.
- **Muscular endurance:** The ability to repeat movements over and over or to hold a particular position for a prolonged period. With greater endurance, it is less likely your body will feel sore after exercising.

- **Flexibility:** The ability to move a joint easily through its full range of motion. Flexibility is particularly important in avoiding injuries.
- **Body composition:** The percentage of the body that is fat.

In addition, physical fitness for a particular sport or activity might include coordination, speed, agility, balance, skill, and other performance-related factors.

Racquetball is an excellent sport for developing all the components of fitness, particularly if you are a fairly skilled player and engage in intense and vigorous play. However, to maximize all of the different components, you should create a program that includes exercises designed specifically to develop each one. Examples are suggested below.

CARDIORESPIRATORY ENDURANCE

Exercises that condition your heart and lungs should have a central role in your fitness program. The best exercises are those that stress a large portion of the body's muscle mass for a prolonged period of time. These include walking, jogging, running, swimming, bicycling, and aerobic dancing. As mentioned above, sports such as racquetball are also good if the skill level and intensity of the game are high enough to provide a vigorous workout. Singles or cutthroat (for the player playing without a team member) provide a more strenuous workout than doubles.

The optimal workout schedule for endurance training is three to five days per week. You may want to begin with three and work up slowly to five to help avoid injury. The activity you choose should be intense enough to raise your heart rate to your target level for cardiorespiratory benefit. Your target heart rate will be approximately seventy to eighty-five percent of your maximum heart rate, which can be approximated by subtracting your age from 220. (For example, if you are twenty-five years old, your target heart rate will be seventy to eighty-five percent of 195, or 137 to 166 beats per minute.)

The length of time you should spend on a workout depends on its intensity. If you are walking slowly or playing a stop-and-start game, you should participate for forty-five to sixty minutes. High-intensity exercise such as running can be practiced for from fifteen to twenty minutes. You should start with less vigorous activities and only gradually increase their intensity.

MUSCULAR STRENGTH AND ENDURANCE

You can improve your muscular strength and endurance with progressive resistance exercises. These include calisthenics, lifting free weights, and weight training with machines. The resistance can be your own body or the weight you are lifting. You can increase your strength by using heavy resistance with few repetitions. If you use lighter resistance and do more repetitions, you improve your muscular endurance. Both strength and endurance are important in racquetball.

Playing racquetball does develop muscular strength and endurance to some degree, but because you use one side of your body more than the other, you may want to add exercises to your exercise program that develop these fitness components on both sides of your body equally. The sample weight training program presented below will help develop many of the muscle groups important in playing racquetball.

You should train at least twice a week for an hour to experience significant results, but allow two to four days' recovery time between workouts. Start with three sets of ten repetitions of each exercise. Choose a starting weight that you can move easily at least ten times; add weight gradually.

1. *Bench press.* Lying on a bench on your back with your feet on the floor, grasp the bar at shoulder width with your palms facing up and away from your body. Lower the bar to your chest (don't bounce), and then return it to the starting position. The bar should follow an elliptical path, during which the weight moves from a low point at the chest to a high point over the eyes.

2. *Lat pulls.* (Lat pulls require the use of a lat machine. If one is not available, substitute pull-ups, chin-ups, or behind-the-neck pull-ups.) From a seated or kneeling position, grasp the bar of the lat machine with palms facing away from yourself and arms fully extended. Pull the weight down until it reaches near the back of your neck, then return to the starting position.

3. *Standing barbell curls.* From a standing position, grasp the bar with your palms upward, your hands shoulder width apart. Keeping your upper body still, bend your

elbows until the bar reaches a level slightly below the collarbone. Return the bar to the starting position. Be sure not to arch your back during this exercise.

4. *Triceps extensions*. Lie on a bench, grasping a barbell with palms facing away from you with your hands from six to twelve inches apart. Push the weight above your chest until your elbows are extended (starting position). Keeping your elbows in a fixed position, carefully lower the weight until it touches your forehead, then push the weight back to the starting position.

5. *Abdominal curls*. Lie on your back on the floor and place your feet on a bench or extend your legs up a wall. With your arms folded across your chest, curl your trunk toward your knees by raising your head and shoulders off the ground. Your back should remain stationary. The resistance can be increased by holding a weight on your chest.

6. *Squats*. Begin standing with your feet shoulder width apart and toes pointed slightly outward with the barbell resting on the back of your shoulders and with your hands holding the bar in that position. Keep your head up and lower back straight. Squat down while maintaining control of your motion until your thighs are approximately parallel with the floor and your gluteals are about one inch below the knee. Drive upward toward the starting position, keeping your back in a fixed position throughout the exercise. Go down slow and up fast.

7. *Calf raises*. Standing on the edge of a stair or block of wood with a barbell resting on your shoulders, slowly lower your heels as far as possible, then raise them until you are up on your toes.

8. *Rotator cuff exercises*. First, lie on your side on a table, with your head propped up on one elbow. Grasp a weight in your free hand and bend your other elbow halfway (ninety degrees) with your free arm perpendicular to the table and your elbow close to your rib cage. Slowly lower the weight, then lift it back to the starting position. Alternate sides.

Next, lie on your back on a table with your elbow bent halfway (ninety degrees) and held close to your side, with your hand holding a weight extended directly above you. Slowly lower the weight to your side by straightening your arm, and then slowly lift it back to the starting position. Alternate sides.

9. *Empty can exercise.* Stand upright and hold a dumbbell in each hand. Keeping your arms straight, raise them to the side to shoulder height, move them inward about thirty degrees, and rotate them down as if you were emptying liquid from two cans. Slowly lower and raise the weight through a forty-five-degree arc.

10. *Wrist extensions.* Use a barbell or dumbbells. In a seated position, with forearms resting on your thigh, hands extending over the edge of your knees, and palms facing you, lower the weight as far as possible, then lift your hands upward by bending at the wrists as much as possible. Repeat this exercise with your grip reversed (palms facing away).

FLEXIBILITY

Flexibility involves stretching movements that gradually increase the length of a muscle or tendon, thus increasing your range of motion. Flexibility is critical in preventing injuries. It is important to stretch at least three to five times a week. You can do flexibility exercises before or after endurance exercise as part of a warm-up or cool-down, or you can set apart a special time for them. (You may develop more flexibility if you do them after exercise, because your muscles are warmer then and can be stretched farther.)

Each exercise should be performed statically; bouncing is dangerous and counterproductive. Stretch to the point of tightness in the muscle and hold the position for ten to thirty seconds. You should feel a pleasant, mild stretch as you let the muscles relax; stretching shouldn't be painful.

1. *Shoulder blade scratch.* Reach back with one arm as if to scratch your shoulder blade. Use your other hand to extend the stretch. Alternate arms.

2. *Towel stretch.* Grasp a rolled towel at both ends in front of you, slowly bring it back over your head, and then lower it as far as possible. Keep your arms straight. (The closer your hands are, the greater the stretch.)

3. *Alternate and double knee-to-chest.* Lying flat on your back, bring one knee up to your chest. Keeping the other leg on the floor, curl your head toward your knee. Return head and leg to the floor, then repeat the procedure, alternating bent legs. Then bring both knees up to your chest and curl your head up to them.

4. *Sole stretch.* Sitting with the soles of your feet pressed together, pull your feet toward you while pressing your knees down with your elbows.

5. *Seated toe touch.* Sit with your legs straight. Bend one leg and fold it up in front of you so that the sole of the foot of your bent leg rests next to your inner thigh, then gradually reach for the toes of your other foot. Alternate legs.

6. *Prone knee flexion.* Lying on your side with one arm tucked behind your head, use the other arm to slowly pull one foot up toward your buttocks. Flex the leg up until you feel the stretch in your quadriceps.

7. *Wall lean.* Stand several feet away from a wall and step forward with one foot (brace yourself against the wall with your forearms). Keep your back straight and your heels on the floor. Bend the knee of the straight leg to change the stretch from the calf muscle to the Achilles tendon. Alternate legs.

8. *Stride stretch.* Assume the racer's starting position and stretch one leg backward. Keep your head down. Alternate legs.

BODY COMPOSITION

The control of body fat is determined by the balance of energy in the body: If more calories are consumed than are expended through metabolism and exercise, then fat increases; if the reverse is true, fat is lost. The best way to control body fat is to follow a diet containing adequate but not excessive calories and to participate in endurance exercise.

Your diet should stress complex carbohydrates (such as fresh fruits and vegetables), and you should limit your intake of fats and sugars. Drink water before and during exercise to prevent dehydration and enhance athletic performance. As a rule of thumb, try to drink about eight ounces of water for every thirty minutes of heavy exercise.

TRAINING IN SPECIFIC SKILLS

A final element in your fitness program is learning the skills required in the sports or activities in which you choose to participate. You can increase your skill as a racquetball player by practicing the drills presented in this text. Once you have mastered the basic skills, alternate drills with practice games to make your workouts more enjoyable and to learn basic strategy.

WARM-UP

Warming up before each practice session or game will help you perform better and prevent injuries. To prepare your body for activity, start with several minutes of calisthenics, fast walking, slow jogging, or any other activity that will accelerate your heart and breathing rates. Once your muscles are warm, you can begin stretching. For exercises done in a standing position, place your feet shoulder-width apart. All stretches should be held, without bouncing, for at least from ten to thirty seconds.

1. *Head circles*. With neck muscles relaxed, roll your head in a full circle. Be sure to maintain good posture and do not force your neck to arch or hyperextend.

2. *Shoulder shrugs*. Elevate your shoulders to ear level and then press them down. Lift both shoulders together and then one shoulder at a time.

3. *Arm circles*. With arms held out to the side, swing your arms in a circle. Begin with small movements, gradually increasing the size of your circles. Repeat in the opposite direction.

4. *Reach stretch*. Reach up toward the ceiling with one arm, fully stretching your side and rib cage. Repeat on the other side.

5. *Side stretch*. Standing with your feet slightly apart and your knees slightly bent, twist your upper body above your waist, alternating sides.

6. *Bent leg reach-through stretch*. Standing in a wide straddle position with your feet parallel, bend your knees and reach through your legs. Perform this stretch slowly, with neck and head relaxed.

7. *Hamstring and Achilles tendon stretches*.

    a. With feet together and parallel and knees bent, bend over and place your hands on or near the floor. Fully bend your knees, lifting your heels as high off the floor as possible.

b. Next, return your heels to the floor and straighten your legs while keeping your hands on the floor. (Keep your knees slightly bent in the forward stretch position.)

c. Beginning in the forward stretch position, walk your hands as far away from your feet as possible, keeping your heels in contact with the floor and your back flat. Hold this position.

d. In the hand-walk position, bend your right knee, lifting your heel off the floor while the heel of your left leg remains on the floor. Reverse the position by lifting your left heel and pressing your right leg straight and your right heel to the floor. Alternate between your right and left legs until your Achilles tendons feel adequately stretched.

8. *Side lunge stretch.* Stand with your legs in a wide straddle, turned out from your hip joint. Lunge by bending one knee and keeping your other leg straight. Place your hands on the floor in front of you for balance. Don't bend your knee past ninety degrees. Repeat for the other leg.

9. *Calf stretch.* Starting with your feet together and parallel, step forward with one foot so that your feet are approximately one to two feet apart. Keeping your back leg straight and toes pointing forward, lunge onto your front leg. Both heels should remain on the floor. Repeat for the other leg.

10. *Ankle circles.* While standing or sitting, raise your right foot off the floor and slowly circle your right ankle clockwise, then counterclockwise. Repeat with the other ankle.

After your warm-up, your muscles should be loose and ready to move.

COOL-DOWN

The cool-down prepares the body for rest, just as the warm-up prepares the body for action. The cool-down is a continuation of the activity you have been doing, but at a lower intensity. Walking and stretching are good activities to perform during a cool-down. The flexibility and warm-up exercises presented above are all appropriate for your cool-down. The amount of time needed for cool-down varies with each individual, but you should plan for at least five minutes.

Rules

4 — PLAY REGULATIONS

Rule 4.1. SERVE

The player or team winning the coin toss has the option to serve or receive for the start of the first game. The second game will begin in reverse order of the first game. The player or team scoring the highest total of points in games 1 and 2 will have the option to serve or receive first at the start of the tiebreaker. In the event that both players or teams score an equal number of points in the first two games, another coin toss will take place and the winner of the toss will have the option to serve or receive.

Rule 4.2. START

The server may not start the service motion until the referee has called the score or "second serve." The serve is started from any place within the service zone. (Certain drive serves are an exception, see Rule 4.6.) Neither the ball nor any part of either foot may extend beyond either line of the service zone when initiating the service motion. Stepping on, but not over, the lines is permitted. When completing the service motion, the server may step over the service (front) line provided that some part of both feet remain on or inside the line until the served ball passes the short line. The server may not step over the short line until the ball passes the short line. See Rules 4.10(a) and 4.11(k) for penalties for violations.

Rule 4.3. MANNER

After taking a set position inside the service zone, a player may begin the service motion — any continuous movement which results in the ball being served. Once the service motion begins, the ball must be bounced on the floor in the zone and be struck by the racquet before it bounces a second time. After being struck, the ball must hit the front wall first and on the rebound hit the floor beyond the back edge of the short line, either with or without touching one of the side walls.

Rule 4.4. READINESS

Serves shall not begin until the referee has called the score or the second serve and the server has visually checked the receiver. The referee shall call the score as both server and receiver prepare to return to their respective position, shortly after the previous rally has ended.

Rule 4.5. DELAYS

Except as noted in Rule 4.5(b), delays exceeding 10 seconds shall result in an out if the server is the offender or a point if the receiver is the offender.

(a) The 10-second rule is applicable to the server and receiver simultaneously. Collectively, they are allowed up to 10 seconds, after the score is called, to serve or be ready to receive. It is the server's responsibility to look and be certain the receiver is ready. If the receiver is not ready, he must signal so by raising his racquet above his head or completely turning his back to the server. (These are the only two acceptable signals.)

(b) If the server serves the ball while the receiver is signaling *not ready*, the serve shall go over with no penalty and the server shall be warned by the referee to check the receiver. If the server continues to serve without checking the receiver, the referee may award a technical for delay of the game.

(c) After the score is called, if the server looks at the receiver and the receiver is not signaling *not ready*, the server may then serve. If the receiver attempts to signal *not ready* after that point, the signal shall not be acknowledged and the serve becomes legal.

Rule 4.6. DRIVE SERVICE ZONES

The drive serve lines will be three feet from each side wall in the service box, dividing the service area into two 17-foot service zones for drive serves only. The player may drive serve to the same side of the court on which he is standing so long as the start and finish of the service motion takes place outside the three-foot line. The call, or non-call, may be appealed.

(a) The drive serve zones are not observed for crosscourt drive serves, the hard-Z, soft-Z, lob, or half-lob serves.

(b) The racquet may not break the plane of the 17-foot zone while making contact with the ball.

(c) The three-foot line is not part of the 17-foot zone. Dropping the ball on the line or standing on the line while serving to the same side is an infraction.

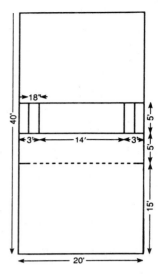

Rule 4.7.   SERVE IN DOUBLES

(a) **Order of Serve.** Each team shall inform the referee of the order of service which shall be followed throughout that game. The order of serve may be changed between games. At the beginning of each game, when the first server of the first team to serve is out, the team is out. Thereafter, both players on each team shall serve until the team receives a handout and a sideout.

(b) **Partner's Position.** On each serve, the server's partner shall stand erect with back to the side wall and with both feet on the floor within the service box from the moment the server begins service motion until the served ball passes the short line. Violations are called *foot faults*. However, if the server's partner enters the safety zone before the ball passes the short line the server loses service.

Rule 4.8.   DEFECTIVE SERVES

Defective serves are of three types, resulting in penalties as follows:

(a) **Dead-Ball Serve.** A dead-ball serve results in no penalty and the server is given another serve (without canceling a prior fault serve).

(b) **Fault Serve.** Two fault serves result in a handout.

(c) **Out Serve.** An out serve results in a handout.

Rule 4.9.   DEAD-BALL SERVES

Dead-ball serves do not cancel any previous fault serve. The following are dead-ball serves:

(a) **Ball Hits Partner.** A serve which strikes the server's partner while in the doubles box is a dead-ball serve. A serve which touches the floor before touching the server's partner is a short serve.

(b) **Court Hinders.** A serve that takes an irregular bounce because it hit a wet spot or an irregular surface on the court is a deadball serve. Also, any serve that hits any surface designated by local rules as an obstruction.

(c) **Broken Ball.** If the ball is determined to have broken on the serve, a new ball shall be substituted and the serve shall be replayed, not canceling any prior fault serve.

Rule 4.10. FAULT SERVES

The following serves are faults and any two in succession result in an out:

(a) **Foot Faults.** A foot fault results when:

(1) The server does not begin the service motion with both feet in the service zone.

(2) The server steps completely over the service line (no part of the foot on or inside the service zone) before the served ball crosses the short line.

(3) In doubles, the server's partner is not in the service box with both feet on the floor and back to the wall from the time the server begins the service motion until the ball passes the short line. (See Rule 4.7.(b).)

(b) **Short Service.** A short serve is any served ball that first hits the front wall and, on the rebound, hits the floor on or in front of the short line (with or without touching a side wall).

(c) **Three-Wall Serve.** A three-wall serve is any served ball that first hits the front wall and, on the rebound, strikes both side walls before touching the floor.

(d) **Ceiling Serve.** A ceiling serve is any served ball that first hits the front wall and then touches the ceiling (with or without touching a side wall).

(e) **Long Serve.** A long serve is a served ball that first hits the front wall and rebounds to the back wall before touching the floor (with or without touching a side wall).

(f) **Out-of-Court Serve.** An out-of-court serve is any served ball that first hits the wall and, before striking the floor, goes out of the court.

(g) **Bouncing Ball Outside Service Zone.** Bouncing the ball outside the service zone as a part of the service motion is a fault serve.

(h) **Illegal Drive Serve.** A drive serve in which the player fails to observe the 17-foot drive service zone outlined in Rule 4.6.

(i) **Screen Serve.** A served ball that first hits the front wall and on the rebound passes so closely to the server, or server's partner in doubles, that it prevents the receiver from having a clear view of the ball. (The receiver is obligated to place himself in good court position, near center court, to obtain that view.) The screen serve is the only fault serve which may not be appealed.

Rule 4.11. OUT SERVES

Any of the following serves results in an out:

(a) **Two Consecutive Fault Serves.** See Rule 4.10.

(b) **Failure to Serve.** Failure of server to put the ball into play under Rule 4.5.

(c) **Missed Serve Attempt.** Any attempt to strike the ball that results in a total miss or in the ball touching any part of the server's body. Also, allowing the ball to bounce more than once during the service motion.

(d) **Touched Serve.** Any served ball that on the rebound from the front wall touches the server or server's racquet, or any ball intentionally stopped or caught by the server or server's partner.

(e) **Fake or Balk Serve.** Any movement of the racquet toward the ball during the serve which is noncontinuous and done for the purpose of deceiving the receiver. If a balk serve occurs, but the referee believes that no deceit was involved, he has the option of declaring "no serve" and having the serve replayed without penalty.

(f) **Illegal Hit.** An illegal hit includes contacting the ball twice, carrying the ball, or hitting the ball with the handle of the racquet or part of the body or uniform.

(g) **Non-Front Wall Serve.** Any served ball that does not strike the front wall first.

(h) **Crotch Serve.** Any served ball that hits the crotch of the front wall and floor, front wall and side wall, or front wall and ceiling is an out serve (because it did not hit the front wall first). A serve into the crotch of the back wall and floor is a good serve and in play. A served ball that hits the crotch of the side wall and floor beyond the short line is in play.

(i) **Out-of-Order Serve.** In doubles, when either partner serves out-of-order, the points scored by that server will be subtracted and an out serve will be called: if the second server serves out-of-order, the out serve will be applied to the first server and the second server will resume serving. If the player designated as the first server serves out-of-order, a sideout will be called. In a match with line judges, the referee may enlist their aid to recall the number of points scored out-of-order.

(j) **Ball Hits Partner.** A served ball that hits the doubles partner while outside the doubles box results in loss of serve.

(k) **Safety Zone Violation.** If the server, or doubles partner, enters into the safety zone before the served ball passes the short line, it shall result in the loss of serve.

Rule 4.12. RETURN OF SERVE

(a) **Receiving Position.**

    (1) The receiver may not enter the safety zone until the ball bounces or crosses the receiving line.

    (2) On the fly return attempt, the receiver may not strike the ball until the ball breaks the plane of the receiving line. The receiver's follow-through may carry the receiver or his racquet past the receiving line.

    (3) Neither the receiver nor his racquet may break the plane of the short line, except if the ball is struck after rebounding off the back wall.

    (4) Any violation by the receiver results in a point for the server.

(b) **Defective Serve.** A player on the receiving side may not intentionally catch or touch a served ball (such as an apparently long or short serve) until the referee has made a call or the ball has touched the floor for a second time. Violation results in a point.

(c) **Legal Return.** After a legal serve, a player on the receiving team must strike the ball on the fly or after the first bounce, and before the ball touches the floor the second time; and return the ball to the front wall, either directly or after touching one or both side walls, the back wall or the ceiling, or any combination of those surfaces. A returned ball must touch the front wall before touching the floor.

(d) **Failure to Return.** The failure to return a serve results in a point for the server.

Rule 4.13. CHANGES OF SERVE

(a) **Outs.** A server is entitled to continue serving until:

    (1) Out Serve. See Rule 4.11.

    (2) Two Consecutive Fault Serves. See Rule 4.10.

    (3) Ball Hits Partner. Player hits partner with attempted return.

    (4) Failure to Return Ball. Player, or partner, fails to keep the ball in play as required by Rule 4.12.(c).

    (5) Avoidable Hinder. Player or partner commits an avoidable hinder which results in an out. See Rule 4.16.

(b) **Sideout.** In singles, retiring the server is a sideout. In doubles the side is retired when both partners have lost service, except: the team which serves first at the beginning of each game loses serve when the first server is retired. (See Rule 4.7.)

(c) **Effect of Sideout.** When the server (or the serving team) receives a sideout, the server becomes the receiver and the receiver becomes the server.

Rule 4.14. RALLIES

All of the play which occurs after the successful return of serve is called the rally. Play shall be conducted according to the following rules:

(a) **Legal Hits.** Only the head of the racquet may be used at any time to return the ball. The racquet may be held in one or both hands. Switching hands to hit a ball, touching the ball with any part of the body or uniform, or removing the wrist thong results in a loss of the rally.

(b) **One Touch.** The player or team trying to return the ball may touch or strike the ball only once or else the rally is lost. The ball may not be *carried*. (A carried ball is one which rests on the racquet in such a way that the effect is more of a sling or throw than a hit.)

(c) **Failure to Return.** Any of the following constitutes a failure to make a legal return during a rally:

   (1) The ball bounces on the floor more than once before being hit.
   (2) The ball does not reach the front wall on the fly.
   (3) The ball caroms off a player's racquet into a gallery or wall opening without first hitting the front wall.
   (4) A ball which obviously did not have the velocity or direction to hit the front wall strikes another player on the court.
   (5) A ball struck by one player on a team, hits that player or that player's partner.
   (6) Committing a point hinder. (Rule 4.16.)
   (7) Switching hands during a rally.
   (8) Failure to use wrist thong on racquet.
   (9) Touching the ball with the body or uniform.
   (10) Carry or sling the ball with the racquet.

(d) **Effect of Failure to Return.** Violations of rules (a), (b), or (c) above result in a loss of rally. If the serving player or team loses the rally, it is an *out* (handout or sideout). If the receiver loses the rally, it results in a point for the server.

(e) **Return Attempts.**
   (1) In singles, if a player swings at the ball and misses it, the player may continue to attempt to return the ball until it touches the floor for the second time.
   (2) In doubles, if one player swings at the ball and misses it, both partners may make further attempts to return the ball until it touches the floor the second time. Both partners on a side are entitled to return the ball.

(f) **Out-of-Court Ball.**

    (1) After Return. Any ball returned to the front wall which, on the rebound or the first bounce, goes into the gallery or through any opening in a sidewall shall be declared dead and the server shall receive two serves.

    (2) No Return. Any ball not returned to the front wall, but which caroms off a player's racquet into the gallery or into any opening in a sidewall either with or without touching the ceiling, side wall, or back wall, shall be an out for the player failing to make the return, or a point for the opponent.

(g) **Broken Ball.** If there is any suspicion that a ball has broken during a rally, play shall continue until the end of the rally. The referee or any player may request the ball be examined. If the referee decides the ball is broken, the ball will be replaced and the rally replayed. The server will get two serves. The only proper way to check for a broken ball is to squeeze it by hand. (Checking the ball by striking it with a racquet will not be considered a valid check and shall work to the disadvantage of the player or team which struck the ball after the rally.)

(h) **Play Stoppage.**

    (1) If a foreign object enters the court, or any other outside interference occurs, the referee shall stop the play.

    (2) If a player loses a shoe or other properly worn equipment, the referee shall stop the play if the occurrence interferes with ensuing play or player's safety; however, safety permitting, the offensive player is entitled to one opportunity to hit a rally ending shot. (See Rule 14.16.(i).)

(i) **Replays.** Whenever a rally is replayed for any reason, the server is awarded two serves. A previous fault serve is not considered.

Rule 4.15.   DEAD-BALL HINDERS

A rally is replayed without penalty and the server receives two serves whenever a dead-ball hinder occurs.

(a) **Situations.**

    (1) Court Hinders. The referee should stop play immediately whenever the ball hits any part of the court that was designated in advance as a court hinder (such as a door handle). The referee should also stop play (i) when the ball takes an irregular bounce as a result of contacting a rough surface (such as court light or vent) or after striking a wet spot on the floor or wall and (ii) when, in the referee's opinion, the irregular bounce affected the rally. A court hinder is the only type of hinder that is appealable. (See Rule 3.7.(a).)

(2) Ball Hits Opponent. When an opponent is hit by a return shot in flight, it is a dead-ball hinder. If the opponent is struck by a ball which obviously did not have the velocity or direction to reach the front wall, it is not a hinder, and the player that hit the ball will lose the rally. A player who has been hit by the ball can stop play and make the call, though the call must be made immediately and acknowledged by the referee.

(3) Body Contact. If body contact occurs which the referee believes was sufficient to stop the rally, either for the purpose of preventing injury by further contact or because the contact prevented a player from being able to make a reasonable return, the referee shall call a hinder. Incidental body contact in which the offensive player clearly will have the advantage should not be called a hinder, unless the offensive player obviously stops play. Contact with the racquet on the follow-through normally is not considered a dead-ball hinder.

(4) Screen Ball. Any ball rebounding from the front wall so close to the body of the defensive team that it interferes with, or prevents, the offensive player from having clear view of the ball. (The referee should be careful not to make the screen call so quickly that it takes away a good offensive opportunity.) A ball that passes between the legs of the side that just returned the ball is not automatically a screen. It depends on the proximity of the players. Again, the call should work to the advantage of the offensive player.

(5) Backswing Hinder. Any body or racquet contact, on the backswing or en route to or just prior to returning the ball, which impairs the hitter's ability to take a reasonable swing. This call can be made by the player attempting the return, though the call must be made immediately and is subject to the referee's approval. Note the interference may be considered an avoidable hinder. (See Rule 4.16.)

(6) Safety Holdup. Any player about to execute a return who believes he is likely to strike his opponent with the ball or racquet may immediately stop play and request a dead-ball hinder. This call must be made immediately and is subject to acceptance and approval of the referee. (The referee will grant a dead-ball hinder if he believes the holdup was reasonable and the player would have been able to return the shot, and the referee may also call an avoidable hinder if warranted.)

(7) Other Interference. Any other unintentional interference which prevents an opponent from having a fair chance to see or return the ball. Example: When a ball from another court enters the court during a rally or when a referee's call on an adjacent court obviously distracts a player.

(b) **Effect of Hinders.** The referee's call of hinder stops play and voids any situation which follows, such as the ball hitting the player. The only hinders that may be called by a player are described in rules (2), (5), and (6) above, and all of these are subject to the approval of the referee. A dead-ball hinder stops play and the rally is replayed. The server receives two serves.

(c) **Avoidance.** While making an attempt to return the ball, a player is entitled to a fair chance to see and return the ball. It is the responsibility of the side that has just hit the ball to move so the receiving side may go straight to the ball and have an unobstructed view of the ball. In the judgment of the referee, however, the receiver must make a reasonable effort to move towards the ball and have a reasonable chance to return the ball in order for a hinder to be called.

Rule 4.16. AVOIDABLE HINDERS

An avoidable hinder results in the loss of the rally. An avoidable hinder does not necessarily have to be an intentional act and is the result of any of the following:

(a) **Failure to Move.** A player does not move sufficiently to allow an opponent a shot straight to the front wall as well as a cross-court shot which is a shot directly to the front wall at an angle that would cause the ball to rebound directly to the rear corner farthest from the player hitting the ball. Also when a player moves in such a direction that it prevents an opponent from taking either of these shots.

(b) **Stroke Interference.** This occurs when a player moves, or fails to move, so that the opponent returning the ball does not have a free, unimpeded swing. This includes unintentionally moving in the wrong direction which prevents an opponent from making an open offensive shot.

(c) **Blocking.** Moves into a position which blocks the opponent from getting to, or returning, the ball; or in doubles, a player moves in front of an opponent as the player's partner is returning the ball.

(d) **Moving into the Ball.** Moves in the way and is struck by the ball just played by the opponent.

(e) **Pushing.** Deliberately pushes or shoves opponent during a rally.

(f) **Intentional Distractions.** Deliberate shouting, stamping of feet, waving of racquet, or any other manner of disrupting one's opponent.

(g) **View Obstruction.** A player moves across an opponent's line of vision just before the opponent strikes the ball.

(h) **Wetting the Ball.** The players, particularly the server, should ensure that the ball is dry prior to the serve. Any wet ball that is not corrected prior to the serve shall result in an avoidable hinder against the server.

(i) **Equipment.** The loss of any improperly worn equipment, or equipment not required on court, which interferes with the play of the ball or safety of the players is an avoidable hinder. Examples of this include the loss of improperly fastened eyewear and hand towels. (See Rule 4.14.(h).)

Rule 4.17. TIMEOUTS

(a) **Rest Periods.** Each player or team is entitled to three 30-second timeouts in games to 15 and two 30-second timeouts in games to 11. Timeouts may not be called by either side after service motion has begun. Calling for a timeout when none remain or after service motion has begun, or taking more than 30 seconds in a timeout, will result in the assessment of a technical for delay of game.

(b) **Injury.** If a player is injured during the course of a match as a result of contact, such as with the ball, racquet, wall, or floor, he will be awarded in injury timeout. While a player may call more than one timeout for the same injury or for additional injuries which occur during the match, a player is not allowed more than a total of 15 minutes of rest during a match. If the injured player is not able to resume play after total rest of 15 minutes, the match shall be awarded to the opponent. Muscle cramps and pulls, fatigue, and other ailments that are not caused by direct contact on the court will not be considered an injury.

(c) **Equipment Timeouts.** Players are expected to keep all clothing and equipment in good, playable condition and are expected to use regular timeouts and time between games for adjustment and replacement of equipment. If a player or team is out of timeouts and the referee determines that an equipment change or adjustment is necessary for fair and safe continuation of the match, the referee may award an equipment timeout not to exceed two minutes. The referee may allow additional time under unusual circumstances.

(d) **Between Games.** The rest period between the first two games of a match is two minutes. If a tiebreaker is necessary, the rest period between the second and third game is five minutes.

(e) **Postponed Games.** Any games postponed by referees shall be resumed with the same score as when postponed.

Rule 4.18. TECHNICALS

(a) **Technical Fouls.** The referee is empowered to deduct one point from a player's or team's score when, in the referee's sole judgment, the player is being overtly and deliberately abusive. The actual invoking of this penalty is called a Referee's Technical. If the player or team against whom the technical was assessed does not resume play immediately, the referee is empowered to forfeit the match in favor of the opponent. Some examples of actions which may result in technicals are:

(1) Excessive arguing.
(2) Threat of any nature to opponent or referee.
(3) Excessive or hard striking of the ball between rallies.
(4) Slamming of the racquet against walls or floor, slamming the door, or any action which might result in injury to the court or other players.
(5) Delay of game. Examples include (i) serving before the receiver is ready, (ii) taking too much time to dry the court, (iii) questioning of the referee excessively about the rules, (iv) exceeding the time allotted for timeouts or between games, or (v) calling a timeout when none remain.
(6) Intentional front line foot faults to negate a bad lob serve.
(7) Anything considered to be unsportsmanlike behavior.
(8) Failure to wear lensed eyewear designed for racquet sports is an automatic technical on the first infraction, and a mandatory timeout will be charged against the offending player to acquire the proper eyewear. A second infraction by that player during the match will result in automatic forfeiture of the match.

(b) **Technical Warning.** If a player's behavior is not so severe as to warrant a referee's technical, a technical warning may be issued without point deduction.

(c) **Effect of Technical or Warning.** If a referee issues a referee's technical, one point shall be removed from the offender's score. If a referee issues a technical warning, it shall not result in a loss of rally or point and shall be accompanied by a brief explanation of the reason for the warning. The awarding of the technical shall have no effect on service changes or sideouts. If the technical occurs either between games or when the offender has no points, the result will be that the offender's score will revert to a minus (-1).

Rule 4.19. PROFESSIONAL

A professional is defined as any player who has accepted prize money regardless of the amount in any PRO SANCTIONED (including WPRA and RMA) tournament or in any other tournament so deemed by the AARA board of directors. (Note: Any player concerned about the adverse effect of losing amateur status should contact the AARA National Office at the earliest opportunity to ensure a clear understanding of this rule and that no action is taken that could jeopardize that status.)

(a) An amateur player may participate in a PRO SANCTIONED tournament but will not be considered a professional (i) if no prize money is accepted or (ii) if the prize money received remains intact and is placed in trust under AARA guidelines.

(b) The acceptance of merchandise or travel expenses shall not be considered prize money, and thus does not jeopardize a player's amateur status.

Rule 4.20. RETURN TO AMATEUR STATUS

Any player who has been classified as a professional can recover amateur status by requesting, in writing, this desire to be reclassified as an amateur. This application shall be tendered to the Executive Director of the AARA or his designated representative, and shall become effective immediately as long as the player making application for reinstatement of amateur status has received no money in any tournament, as defined in Rule 4.19, for the past 12 months.

Rule 4.21. AGE GROUP DIVISIONS

Age is determined as of the first day of the tournament:

(a) **Men's and Women's Age Divisions:**
Open — All players other than Pro
Junior Veterans — 19 +
Junior Veterans — 25 +
Veterans — 30 +
Seniors — 35 +
Veteran Seniors — 40 +
Masters — 45 +
Veteran Masters — 50 +
Golden Masters — 55 +
Senior Golden Masters — 60 +
Veteran Golden Masters — 65 +
Advanced Golden Masters — 70 +
Super Golden Masters — 75 +
Grand Masters — 80 +

(b) **Other Divisions.**
Doubles
Mixed Doubles
Wheelchair
Visually Impaired

(c) **Junior Divisions.** Age determined as of January 1st of each calendar year. Junior Boy's and Girl's age divisions:
18 & Under
16 & Under
14 & Under

12 & Under
10 & Under
8 & Under
8 & Under Multi-Bounce
Doubles
Mixed Doubles

Rule 4.22. EIGHT AND UNDER MULTI-BOUNCE MODIFICATIONS

In general, the AARA's standard rules governing racquetball play will be followed except for the modifications which follow.

(a) **Basic Return Rule.** In general, the ball remains in play as long as it is bouncing. However, the player may swing only once at the ball and the ball is considered dead at the point it stops bouncing and begins to roll. Also, anytime the ball rebounds off the back wall, it must be struck before it crosses the short line en route to the front wall, except as explained in the Blast Rule.

(b) **Blast Rule.** If the ball caroms from the front wall to the back wall on the fly, the player may hit the ball from any place on the court — including past the short line — so long as the ball is bouncing.

(c) **Front Wall Lines.** Two parallel lines (tape may be used) should be placed across the front wall such that the bottom edge of one line is three feet above the floor and the bottom edge of the other line is one foot above the floor. During the rally, any ball that hits the front wall (i) below the three-foot line and (ii) either on or above the one-foot line must be returned before it bounces a third time. However, if the ball hits below the one-foot line, it must be returned before it bounces twice. If the ball hits on or above the three-foot line, the ball must be returned as described in the basic return rule.

(d) **Games and Matches.** All games are played to 11 points, and the first side to win two games wins the match.

5 — TOURNAMENTS

Rule 5.1. DRAWS

(a) If possible, all draws shall be made at least two days before the tournament commences. The seeding method of drawing shall be approved by the AARA.

(b) The draw and seeding committee shall be chaired by the AARA's Executive Director, National Commissioner, and the host tournament director. No other persons shall participate in the draw or seeding unless at the invitation of the draw and seeding committee.

(c) In local and regional tournaments the draw shall be the responsibility of the tournament director. In regional play, the tournament director should work in coordination with the AARA Regional Commissioner at the tournament.

Rule 5.2.   SCHEDULING

(a) **Preliminary Matches.** If one or more contestants are entered in both singles and doubles, they may be required to play both singles and doubles on the same day or night with little rest between matches. This is a risk assumed on entering two singles events or a singles and doubles event. If possible, the schedule should provide at least a one-hour rest period between matches.

(b) **Final Matches.** Where one or more players has reached the finals in both singles and doubles, it is recommended that the doubles match be played on the day preceding the singles. This would assure more rest between the final matches. If both final matches must be played on the same day or night, the following procedure is recommended:

(1) The singles match be played first.
(2) A rest period of not less than one hour be allowed between the finals in singles and doubles.

Rule 5.3.   NOTICE OF MATCHES

After the first round of matches, it is the responsibility of each player to check the posted schedules to determine the time and place of each subsequent match. If any change is made in the schedule after posting, it shall be the duty of the committee or tournament director to notify the players of the change.

Rule 5.4.   THIRD PLACE

Players are not required to play off for 3rd place or 4th place. However, for point standings, if one semifinalist wants to play off for third and the other semifinalist does not, the one willing to play shall be awarded third place. If both semifinalists do not wish to play off for 3rd or 4th position, then the points shall be awarded evenly.

Rule 5.5.   ROUND ROBIN SCORING

The position of players or teams in round robin competition is determined by the following sequence:

(a) Winner of the most matches;

(b) In a two-way tie, winner of the head-to-head match prevails;

(c) In a tie of three or more, the player who lost the fewest games is awarded the highest position:

   (1) If a two-way tie results, revert to No. 2;
   (2) If a multiple tie remains, total points scored against the player in all matches will be tabulated. The player with the least points scored against will prevail.

   Note: Forfeits will count as a match won in two games. In cases where points scored against is the tiebreaker, the points scored by the forfeiting team will be discounted from consideration of points scored against all teams.

Rule 5.6. AARA REGIONAL TOURNAMENTS

The United States and Europe are divided into 16 regions as specified in rule 5.11.(c).

(a) A player may compete in only one regional singles and one regional doubles tournament per year.

(b) The defined area of eligibility for a person's region is that of their permanent residence. Players are encouraged to participate in their own region; however, for the purpose of convenience players may participate outside their region.

(c) A player can participate in only two championship events in a regional tournament.

(d) Awards and remuneration to the AARA National Championships will be posted on the entry blank.

Rule 5.7. TOURNAMENT MANAGEMENT

In all AARA sanctioned tournaments, the tournament director and/or the national AARA official in attendance may decide on a change of court after the completion of any tournament game, if such a change will accommodate better spectator conditions.

Rule 5.8 TOURNAMENT CONDUCT

In all AARA sanctioned tournaments, the referee is empowered to default a match, if the conduct of a player or team is considered detrimental to the tournament and the game. (See Rule 3.5.(d) and 3.5.(e).)

Rule 5.9. AARA ELIGIBILITY

(a) Any current AARA member who has not been classified as a professional (see Rule 4.19) may compete in any AARA sanctioned tournament.

(b) Any current AARA member who has been classified as a professional may compete in any AARA sanctioned event that offers prize money or merchandise.

Rule 5.10. DIVISION COMPETITION

Men and women may compete only in events for their respective sex during Regional and National Championships. If there is not a sufficient number of players to warrant play in a specific division, the tournament director may place the entrants in a comparably competitive division. Note: For the purpose of encouraging the development of women's racquetball, the governing bodies of numerous states permit women to play in the men's division when a comparable skill level isn't available in the women's division.

Rule 5.11. U.S. NATIONAL CHAMPIONSHIPS

The National Singles, Junior, and National Doubles are separate tournaments and are played on different weekends. There will be a consolation round in all divisions.

(a) **Regional Qualifications.**

   (1) The National Ratings Committee may handle the rating of each region and determine how many players shall qualify from each regional tournament.
   (2) AARA National Champions are exempt from qualifying for the following year's National Championship.
   (3) There may be a tournament one day ahead of the National Tournament at the same site to qualify 8 players in each division who were unable to qualify or who failed to qualify in the Regionals. This rule is in force only when a region is obviously over subscribed.

(b) **Definition of Regions.**

   (1) Qualifying Singles. A player may have to qualify at one of the 17 regional tournaments.
   (2) Qualifying Doubles. There will be no regional qualifying for doubles.

(c) **AARA Regions.**

   (1) Maine, New Hampshire, Vermont, Massachusetts, Rhode Island, Connecticut
   (2) New York, New Jersey
   (3) Pennsylvania, Maryland, Virginia, Delaware, District of Columbia
   (4) Florida, Georgia
   (5) Alabama, Mississippi, Tennessee
   (6) Arkansas, Kansas, Missouri, Oklahoma
   (7) Texas, Louisiana

(8) Wisconsin, Iowa, Illinois
(9) West Virginia, Ohio, Michigan
(10) Indiana, Kentucky
(11) North Dakota, South Dakota, Minnesota, Nebraska
(12) Arizona, New Mexico, Utah, Colorado
(13) Montana, Wyoming
(14) California, Hawaii, Nevada
(15) Washington, Idaho, Oregon, Alaska
(16) Americans in Europe
(17) North Carolina, South Carolina

Rule 5.12. U.S. NATIONAL JUNIOR OLYMPIC CHAMPIONSHIPS

It will be conducted on a separate date and at a separate location under the same parameters provided in Rules 5.11(a) and 5.11(b).

Rule 5.13. U.S. NATIONAL INTERCOLLEGIATE CHAMPIONSHIPS

It will be conducted on a separate date and at a separate location.

6 — NATIONAL WHEELCHAIR RACQUETBALL ASSOCIATION MODIFICATIONS

Rule 6.1. CHANGES TO STANDARD RULES

In general, the AARA's standard rules governing racquetball play will be followed except for the modifications which follow.

(a) Where the AARA Rulebook rules refer to server, person, body, or other similar variations, for wheelchair play such reference shall include all parts of the wheelchair in addition to the person sitting on it.

(b) Where the rules refer to feet, standing or other similar descriptions, for wheelchair play it means only where the rear wheels actually touch the floor.

(c) Where the rules mention body contact, for wheelchair play it shall mean any part of the wheelchair in addition to the player.

(d) Where the rules refer to *double bounce* or after the first bounce, it shall mean three bounces. All variations of the same phrases shall be revised accordingly.

Rule 6.2. DIVISIONS

(a) **Novice Division.** The Novice Division is for the beginning player who is just learning to play.

(b) **Intermediate Division.** The Intermediate Division is for the player who has played tournaments before and has a skill level to be competitive in the division.

(c) **Open Division.** The Open Division is the highest level of play and is for the advanced player.

(d) **Multi-Bounce Division.** The Multi-Bounce Division is for the individuals (men or women) whose mobility is such that wheel-chair racquetball would be impossible if not for the Multi-Bounce Division.

(e) **Junior Division.** The Junior Divisions are for players who are under the age of 19. The tournament director will determine if the divisions will be played as two-bounce or multi-bounce. Age divisions are: 8–11, 12–15, and 16–18.

Rule 6.3.   RULES

(a) **Two-Bounce Rule.** Two bounces are used in wheelchair racquetball in all divisions except the Multi-Bounce Division. The ball may hit the floor twice before being returned.

(b) **Out of Chair Rule.** The player can neither intentionally jump out of his chair to hit a ball nor stand up in his chair to serve the ball. If the referee determines that the chair was left intentionally, it will result in loss of the rally for the offender. If a player unintentionally leaves his chair, no penalty will be assessed. Repeat offenders will be warned by the referee.

(c) **Equipment Standards.** In order to protect playing surfaces, the tournament officials may not allow a person to participate with black tires or anything which will mark or damage the court.

(d) **Start.** The serve may be started from any place within the service zone. Although the front casters may extend beyond the lines of the service zone, at no time shall the rear wheels cross either the service or short line before the served ball crosses the short line. Penalties for violation are the same as those for the standard game.

(e) **Maintenance Delay.** A maintenance delay is a delay in the progress of a match due to a malfunction of a wheelchair, prosthesis, or assistive device. Such delay must be requested by the player, granted by the referee during the match, and shall not exceed five minutes. Only two such delays may be granted for each player for each match. After using both maintenance delays the player has the following options:

   (1) Continue play with the defective equipment.
   (2) Immediately substitute replacement equipment.
   (3) Postponement of game, with the approval of the referee and opponent.

Rule 6.4. MULTI-BOUNCE RULES

(a) The ball may bounce as many times as the receiver wants though the player may swing only once to return the ball to the front wall.

(b) The ball must be hit before it crosses the short line on its way back to the front wall.

(c) The receiver cannot cross the short line after the ball contacts the back wall.

7 — VISUALLY IMPAIRED MODIFICATIONS

In general, the AARA's standard rules governing racquetball play will be followed except for the modifications which follow.

Rule 7.1. ELIGIBILITY

A player's visual acuity must not be better than 20/200 with the best practical eye correction or else the player's field of vision must not be better than 20 degrees. The three classifications of blindness are B-1 (totally blind to light perception), B-2 (able to see hand movement up to 20/600 corrected), and B-3 (from 20/600 to 20/200 corrected).

Rule 7.2. RETURN OF SERVE AND RALLIES

On the return of serve and on every return thereafter, the player may make multiple attempts to strike the ball until (i) the ball has been touched, (ii) the ball has stopped bouncing, or (iii) the ball has passed the short line after touching the back wall. The only exception is described in Rule 7.3.

Rule 7.3. BLAST RULE

If the ball (other than on the serve) caroms from the front wall to the back wall on the fly, the player may retrieve the ball from any place on the court — including in front of the short line — so long as the ball has not been touched and is still bouncing.

Rule 7.4. HINDERS

A hinder will result in the rally being replayed without penalty unless the hinder was intentional. If a hinder is clearly an intentional hinder, an avoidable hinder should be called and the rally awarded to the nonoffending player or team.

8—WOMEN'S PROFESSIONAL RACQUETBALL ASSOCIATION MODIFICATIONS

In general, the AARA's standard rules governing racquetball play will be followed except for the modifications which follow.

Rule 8.1.   MATCH, GAME, SUPER TIEBREAKER

A match is won by the first side winning three games. All games, other than the fifth one, are won by the first side to score 11 points. The fifth game, which is called the Super Tiebreaker, is won by the first side scoring 11 points and having at least a two-point lead. If necessary, the game will continue beyond 11 points until such time as one side has a two-point lead.

Rule 8.2.   APPEALS

There is NO limit on the number of appeals that a player or team may make.

Rule 8.3.   SERVE

The server may leave the service zone as soon as the serve has been made.

Rule 8.4.   DRIVE SERVICE ZONE

The server may begin a drive serve anywhere in the service zone so long as the server is completely inside the 17-foot drive service zone when the ball is actually contacted.

Rule 8.5.   RETURN OF SERVE

The receiver may enter the safety zone as soon as the ball has been served. The served ball may not be contacted in the receiving zone until it has bounced. Neither the receiver nor the receiver's racquet may break the plane of the short line unless the ball is struck after rebounding off the back wall. On the fly return attempt, the receiver may not strike the ball until the ball breaks the plane of the receiving line. The receiver's follow-through may carry the receiver or the racquet past the receiving line.

Rule 8.6.   AVOIDABLE HINDER

An avoidable hinder should be called only if the player's movement or failure to move interfered with the opponent's opportunity to take an offensive shot.

Rule 8.7. TIMEOUTS

Each player or team is entitled to two 30-second timeouts per game.

Rule 8.8. TIME BETWEEN GAMES

The rest period between all games will be 2 minutes except that a 5-minute rest period will be allowed between the fourth and fifth games.

9 — ONE-WALL AND THREE-WALL MODIFICATIONS

In general, the AARA's standard rules governing racquetball play will be followed except for the modifications which follow.

(a) **One Wall.** There are two playing surfaces, the front wall and the floor. The wall is 20 feet wide and 16 feet high. The floor is 20 feet wide and 34 feet to the back edge of the long line. To permit movement by players, there should be a minimum of three feet (six feet is recommended) beyond the long line and six feet outside each side line.

   (1) Short Line. The back edge of the short line is 16 feet from the wall.
   (2) Service Markers. Lines at least six inches long which are parallel with, and midway between, the long and short lines. The extension of the service markers form the imaginary boundary of the service line.
   (3) Service Zone. The entire floor area inside and including the short line, side lines, and service line.
   (4) Receiving Zone. The entire floor area in back of the short line, including the side lines and the long line.

(b) **Three Wall with Short Side Wall.** The front wall is 20 feet wide and 20 feet high. The side walls are 20 feet long and 20 feet high, though the side wall tapers down to 12 feet high. The floor length and court markings are the same as four-wall.

(c) **Three Wall with Long Side Wall.** The court is 20 feet wide, 20 feet high, and 40 feet long. The side walls may taper from 20 feet high at the front wall down to 12 feet high at the end of the court. All court markings are the same as four-wall.

(d) **Service in Three Wall Courts.** A serve that goes beyond the side walls on the fly is considered long. A serve that goes beyond the long line on a fly, but within the side walls, is the same as a short.

10–HOW TO REFEREE WHEN THERE IS NO REFEREE

SAFETY IS THE RESPONSIBILITY OF EVERY PLAYER WHO ENTERS THE COURT.

At no time should the physical safety of the participants be compromised. Players are entitled, and expected, to hold up their swing, *without penalty*, any time they believe there might be a risk of physical contact. Any time a player says he held up to avoid contact, even if he was overcautious, he is entitled to hinder (rally replayed without penalty).

SCORE

Since there is no referee, or scorekeeper, it is important for the server to announce both the server's and receiver's score before *every* first serve.

DURING RALLIES

During rallies, it is the *hitter's* responsibility to make the call. If there is a possibility of a skip ball, double-bounce, or illegal hit, play should continue until the hitter makes the call against himself. If the hitter does not make the call against himself and goes on to win the rally, and the player thought that one of the hitter's shots was not good, he may *appeal* to the hitter by pointing out which shot he thought was bad and request the hitter to reconsider. If the hitter is sure of his call, and the opponent is still sure the hitter is wrong, the rally is replayed. As a matter of etiquette, players are expected to make calls against themselves any time they are not sure. Unless the hitter is certain the shot was good, he should call it a skip.

SERVICE

(a) **Fault Serves.** The receiver has the primary responsibility to make these calls, though either player may make the call. The receiver must make the call immediately, and not wait until he hits the ball and has the benefit of seeing how good a shot he can hit. *It is not an option play.* The receiver does not have the right to play a short serve just because he thinks it's a setup.

(b) **Screen Serves.** When there is no referee, the screen serve call is the sole responsibility of the receiver. If the receiver has taken the proper court position, near center court, and does not have clear view of the ball, the screen should be called *immediately*. The receiver may not call a screen after attempting to hit the ball or after taking himself out of proper court position by starting the wrong way. *The server may not call a screen under any circumstances* and must expect to play the rally unless he hears a call from the receiver.

(c) **Other Situations.** Foot faults, 10-second violations, receiving line violations, service zone infringement, and other technical calls really require a referee. However, if either player believes his opponent is abusing any of the rules, be sure there is agreement on what the rule is, and put each other on notice that the rules should be followed.

HINDERS

Generally, the hinder should work like the screen serve — as an option play for the hindered party. *Only the person going for the shot can stop play by calling a hinder, and he must do so immediately* — not wait until he has the benefit of seeing how good a shot he can hit. If the hindered party believes he can make an effective return in spite of some physical contact or screen that has occurred, he may continue to play.

AVOIDABLE HINDERS

Since avoidable hinders are usually unintentional, they can occur even in the friendliest matches. A player who realizes that he caused such a hinder should simply declare his opponent to be the winner of the rally. If a player feels that his opponent caused such a hinder, but the opponent does not make the call on himself, the offended player should point out that he thought an avoidable hinder occurred. However, unless the opponent agrees that a point hinder occurred, none will be called. Often just pointing out what appears to have been a point hinder will prevent the opponent from such actions on future rallies.

DISPUTES

If either player, for any reason, desires to have a referee, it is considered common courtesy for the other player to go along with the request, and a referee suitable to both sides should be found. If there is not a referee and a question about a rule or rule interpretation comes up, seek out the club pro or a more experienced player. Then, after the match, contact your state racquetball association for the answer.

GLOSSARY
· · · · · · ·

Ace   A legal serve that is untouched by the opponent's racquet.

Alley   Two imaginary areas on either side of the court, extending from front to back walls and eighteen inches out from the side walls.

Anticipating   Predicting your opponent's next shot.

Around-the-walls shot   A defensive shot that first hits a side wall, then the front wall, then the other side wall before touching the floor.

Avoidable hinder   Interference with the opponent's play that could have been prevented or avoided.

Backcourt   The last fifteen feet of the court, covering the area from the receiving line to the back wall.

Backhand   A stroke that hits the ball by bringing the racquet across the body.

Backspin   Hitting the ball so that it rotates in the opposite direction.

Backswing   The portion of a swing in which the racquet is brought back in preparation for hitting the ball.

Back wall   The rear wall of the court.

Backwall shot   A shot made on a ball rebounding off the rear wall.

Block   Using your body to obstruct an opponent's ability to get to the ball.

Body contact   Colliding with your opponent; this is sometimes a block when it interferes with an opponent's return.

Bumper guard   The plastic protector at the top of the racquet.

Ceiling shot   A shot that hits the ceiling before hitting the front wall.

Centercourt   The area of the court just behind the short line, midway between the side walls.

Change of pace   A change in the speed of a shot from its former speed.

Controlling centercourt   Returning to centercourt and successfully preventing your opponent from returning there.

Court hinder   When the ball is deflected by an obstruction on the court, such as a door handle or light fixture (the point is replayed).

Crack (crotch)   The point where two surfaces meet each other. For example, the side and front wall, or the side wall and floor.

Crosscourt pass shot   A shot that is hit from one side of the court and that, after hitting the front wall, travels to the opposite side of the court out of reach of the opponent.

Cutthroat   A game involving three players; the server plays against the other two players.

Dead ball   A ball that is no longer in play.

Default   To lose a match by failing to show up or refusing to play.

Defective serve   Any illegal serve.

Defensive shot   A shot made to continue a rally in an attempt to maneuver an opponent out of the centercourt position.

Die   When a ball loses momentum.

Dig   Returning a ball that would have constituted a win for your opponent.

Doubles   A game or match in which one team opposes another team; each team consists of two players.

Down-the-line shot   A shot hit near a side wall that hits the front wall directly and then rebounds back along the same side wall.

Drive   A powerful ball that travels in a straight line.

Drop shot   A shot hit with very little force, rebounding only a few feet from the front wall.

Error   When a player does not return a ball that should have been easily returned.

Eye guards   Special glasses or protectors worn to protect the eyes while playing racquetball.

Fault   An illegal serve or an infraction of the rules while serving (two faults result in a side out).

Float   When the ball travels slowly and appears to hang in the air.

Follow-through   Continuing the swing after making contact with the ball.

Foot fault   An illegal position in which the server's foot is outside the service zone during the serve.

Front/back   *See "I" formation.*

Frontcourt   The first fifteen feet of the court from the front wall to the service line.

Front-wall kill   A kill shot that hits and rebounds off the front wall, touching neither side wall, and then returns so that the opponent is unable to retrieve it.

Game   The portion of a match that is normally completed when one player, or team, reaches 15 points (or any number of points agreed upon by the players). If a third game is necessary, it is usually played to 11 points.

Game point   The final point that can decide the outcome of a game.

Garbage lob serve   A half lob hit halfway up the front wall that rebounds to the receiver at about shoulder height.

Grip   The manner in which the racquet is held.

Half volley   Hitting the ball on the rise, just after it bounces off the floor; the shot resulting from this action.

Handout   Loss of the serve.

Hinder   An unintentional interference or screen of the ball that prevents the opponent from having a fair chance to return the ball (the point is replayed without penalty).

"I" formation   (also called front/back) A method of positioning players for doubles; one player covers the frontcourt, the other the backcourt.

Inning   A round of play that is completed after both teams have served.

Kill shot   An offensive shot that hits the front wall so low that a return by the opponent is impossible.

Live ball   Any ball that is still in play.

Lob shot   A shot hit high and gently toward the front wall, rebounding to the back wall in a high arc.

Long serve   A serve that rebounds to the back wall without hitting the floor (this is a fault).

Match   A period of play that ends when one player, or team, wins two of three games.

Match point   The final point that can decide the outcome of a match.

Midcourt   The area of the court between the service line and the receiving line.

Offensive shot   An aggressive shot designed to win the point as fast as possible.

Out   When a player does not return a ball that is in play.

Out of court   When a serve or return is hit out of the playing area.

Out of order   In doubles, when a player serves out of turn.

Out serve   Any illegal serve (the player loses the serve).

Overhead   A shot hit at shoulder level or higher.

Pass shot   A shot hit past an opponent and out of reach.

Pinch shot   A kill shot that hits the side and front walls near the crack.

Point   A unit used in scoring; a point can only be won by the serving team.

Point of contact   The spot where the ball hits the racquet.

Power serve   A hard-hit serve where the ball rebounds fast to the backcourt.

Rally   An exchange of shots that is continued until the end of play.

Ranking   Player ratings used in tournaments.

Ready position   A stance taken by a player while waiting for a serve or shot.

Receiving line   A mark on the side wall five feet behind the short line.

Right/left   (also called side-by-side) A method of positioning players for doubles; each player covers half the court (either the left or right side).

Roll-out   A shot in which the ball rolls out on the floor after rebounding off the front wall — a sure point because it is impossible to retrieve.

Safety hinder   When play is stopped to prevent a player from being injured.

Safety zone   The area between the short line and the receiving line.

Screen   Interference with the opponent's view of the ball.

Serve   Putting the ball into play; the shot used to accomplish this.

Service line   The front line of the service zone.

Set up   A shot that can easily be returned.

Shooter   A player who tries to kill the ball.

Short line   The back line of the service zone, located at the midpoint of the court.

Side by side   *See Right/left.*

Sideout   The loss of service to the opponent.

Singles   A racquetball game in which one player opposes another player.

Skip ball   A low ball that hits the floor before reaching the front wall.

Straight kill   *See Front-wall kill.*

Three-wall serve   A serve that hits two walls besides the front wall (this is a fault).

Throat   The part of the racquet between the strings and the grip.

Tournament   A formally organized match or series of matches.

Volley   Hitting the ball before it bounces; the shot resulting from this action.

Wallpaper shot   A shot hit close to the side wall so that it is difficult to return.

Winner   A shot that results in a point or side out.

Z-serve   Same as a Z-shot, except that the ball hits the floor before hitting the third wall.

Z-shot   A ball hit high into the front-wall corner that rebounds to the near side wall and then to the opposite side wall.

INDEX
● ● ● ● ● ● ●